Advance Praise fo.

Good Grandpa

"This is by far the best book by Ted Page that I have ever read."

—**John Cleese**

"I can't wait for you to read this book. Whether you are a grandpa, or have loved a grandpa, the stories in these pages will stir something within you: a memory, a desire, or an intention. I wept through several parts, not least because I've watched my own children lose both their grandpas in recent years. Ted has given voice to a role that is often misunderstood—or, too often, made to seem small beside the role of a grandmother. Through storytelling, interviews with grandfathers, and reflections on his own family experiences, he shows us how a grandfather's love and wisdom can—and does—transcend and transform generations. This book is filled with golden nuggets of wisdom—powerful one-liners you'll highlight, pause to reflect on, and likely share with your own family. It's a moving, fun and deeply meaningful read."

—**Kerry Byrne**, PhD, Founder, The Long Distance Grandparent

"*Good Grandpa* offers a fresh, sorely needed perspective into the modern world of grandparenthood. Through touching personal anecdotes and interviews with fascinating real-world grandfathers, Ted Page masterfully weaves a tapestry of what intentional grandparenting looks like from a variety of perspectives, and why it matters now more than ever for today's young families. This book is refreshing, informative, and inspiring. Without a doubt, *Good Grandpa* is a must-read for grandparents of all ages and stages, especially (but not limited to) grandfathers."

—**Aaron Larsen**, Founder, GrandparentsAcademy.com

"There isn't a training program when you become a grandfather. But Ted Page's book curates valuable lessons from grandfathers to give us what we need most—an appreciation of the impact we can have on the next generation."

—**Joe Casey**, *The Retirement Wisdom Podcast*

"*Good Grandpa* is rich with personal stories, generational wisdom, and laugh-out-loud moments that show how cool grandfathers can shape the future while savoring the present. Whether you're a brand-new 'Boppy' or a seasoned pro, this book is your invitation to embrace the role of grandpa with purpose, love, and a lot of heart."

—**Greg Payne**, *The Cool Grandpa Podcast*

"A great book for all grandpas and their families to read and enjoy!"

—**Dr. Jim Isenberg**, Grandpas United

GOOD GRANDPA

GOOD GRANDPA

Stories from the Heart of Grandfatherhood

TED PAGE

A REGALO PRESS BOOK

Good Grandpa:
Stories from the Heart of Grandfatherhood
© 2025 by Ted Page, LLC
All Rights Reserved
Good Grandpa® is a registered trademark.

ISBN: 979-8-88845-505-0
ISBN (eBook): 979-8-88845-506-7

Cover design by Kristin Collins
Interior design and composition by Greg Johnson, Textbook Perfect

Publishing Team:
Founder and Publisher: Gretchen Young
Editorial Assistant: Caitlyn Limbaugh
Managing Editor: Madeline Sturgeon
Production Manager: Kate Harris
Production Editor: Courtney Michaelson

As part of the mission of Regalo Press, a donation is being made to Kim Long Orphanage in Vietnam, as chosen by the author. Find out more about this organization at: https://st-paul-hue.com.

NO AI TRAINING: Without in any way limiting the author's [and publisher's] exclusive rights under copyright, any use of this publication to "train" generative artificial intelligence (AI) technologies to generate text is expressly prohibited. The author reserves all rights to license uses of this work for generative AI training and development of machine learning language models.

This book, as well as any other Regalo Press publications, may be purchased in bulk quantities at a special discounted rate. Contact orders@regalopress.com for more information.

No part of this book may be reproduced, stored in a retrieval system, or transmitted by any means without the written permission of the author and publisher.

Regalo Press
New York • Nashville
regalopress.com

Published in the United States of America
2 3 4 5 6 7 8 9 10

To Tom and the Greatest Generation

"Research my colleagues and I have been conducting indicates that grandparent-aged individuals became common relatively recently in human prehistory and that this change came at about the same time as cultural shifts toward distinctly modern behaviors—including a dependence on sophisticated symbol-based communication of the kind that underpins art and language. These findings suggest that living to an older age had profound effects on the population sizes, social interactions and genetics of early modern human groups and may explain why they were more successful than archaic humans, such as the Neandertals."

—"The Evolution of Grandparents,"
Scientific American

"It's time to make grandpas hip."

—KEITH RICHARDS

Contents

INTRODUCTION xiii

PROLOGUE Fishing Down Between the Mountains 1

CHAPTER 1 You're Boppy! 7

CHAPTER 2 Secrets of the Desk 12

CHAPTER 3 The New Greatest Generation 17

CHAPTER 4 Flight of the Monarchs 27

CHAPTER 5 Labors of Love 38

CHAPTER 6 The Call of Nature 46

CHAPTER 7 Unsilly Wisdom from John Cleese 49

CHAPTER 8 The Fuel 52

CHAPTER 9 Lifeboats in the Starry Night 63

CHAPTER 10 Letters from Saba 72

CHAPTER 11 The Forever Story 81

CHAPTER 12 The Profitable Lemonade Stand 92

CHAPTER 13 A Lab of Their Own 100

CHAPTER 14 The Six Grandfathers 108

CHAPTER 15 The World Next Door 116

CHAPTER 16 Grandma's Karmann Ghia 127

CHAPTER 17 The Kim Long Orphanage 134

CHAPTER 18 Let There Be Light 149

CHAPTER 19 Lost in the Amazon 171

CHAPTER 20 Reaching with the Only Hand You Have for the Brass Ring 183

CHAPTER 21 The Nearly Indescribable Joy and Sadness of Seeing Them Grow Up 191

CHAPTER 22 The Day I Burned the Piano 194
CHAPTER 23 My Number One Thing 203
CHAPTER 24 Dreaming Goodbye 212
EPILOGUE Dear Twenty-Six-Year-Old Us 216
RESOURCES OF NOTE 220
ENDNOTES 223
ACKNOWLEDGMENTS 226
ABOUT THE AUTHOR 229

Introduction

Upon hearing the news of my impending grandfatherhood I was so overwhelmed with happiness I joined my wife, Nancy, in going bananas. I hugged her. I hugged my daughter and son-in-law. I hugged the in-laws. I think I may have hugged our cat while I was at it. But I also suddenly remembered my grandfather, or as we all called him, Gramp.

Gramp made a big impression on me for a lot of reasons. He and my Gram ran the family's summer rental cottage business on Lake Willoughby in Vermont, and they spent their winters across town from our home in Lexington, Massachusetts, so there was plenty of time together. He was a storyteller and a singer. A veteran. A man who believed there was no substitute for hard work.

Gramp was also old.

Well into his seventies when I was a teenager, his face was deeply lined. When he walked or pushed the wheelbarrow around the farm cottages, he was always bent forward at the waist, and as the years progressed, he tended to forget things. Gramp gradually descended into dementia. But right up until his end, he'd walk about in a khaki shirt, pants, and cap, ordering me to do this or that, or regaling me with a story.

Gram and Gramp, 1972.

When I became a grandfather I was only fifty-five. Yet in an instant I was part of the same grandpa club. I didn't really know how to reconcile those two images, the old man and me, into who I was.

So, I hunted for answers on the web. How could I be a good grandpa? All I could find was generic grandparenting websites chock-full of ads for dentures and nursing homes. Or ubiquitous stock photos of older couples walking and laughing on a beach, the husband with a sweater draped over his shoulders, the wife in a coastal grandma outfit (before that was a thing), and both with wide smiles and perfect white teeth. The only prominent cultural reference to grandfathers was the movie *Bad Grandpa.* I love comedy but didn't exactly relate to the senile lecherous drunk in the movie.

Fortunately, having spent most of my career creating and publishing online content for clients of my marketing agency, I had the tools needed to do something different, something I and others could find relevant and entertaining. I started a blog called—you guessed it—*Good Grandpa,* and began writing about my experiences.

Writing for a new blog is a lot like talking to yourself in an empty room. Over time, family members started checking out stories. Then friends joined the party. Then friends of friends. Followed by press articles and a growing readership.

When *The New York Times* featured the blog in their "How to Become a Better Grandpa" story, I was blown away by the hundreds of comments posted on the *Times* website. Again and again, people wrote with great emotion about cherished experiences with their grandpas. Some of the grandpas they wrote about were still with them, and many had passed on and were now fragments of memory, all the more poignant for their brevity. The word used most often was "love."

The other thing that struck me about the *Times* article comments, as well as the many comments I've seen over the years publishing my blog, is the extent to which people's experiences with their grandpas helped guide and shape them into their best adult lives, just as my Gramp helped shape my life.

Yet all the ways we grandfathers have achieved this kind of nurturing, throughout all of human history, have only been passed down by word of mouth, or the occasional story published here or there. The wisdom of grandpas, along with the myriad ways grandpas have found to live their lives to the fullest, has been largely absent from popular culture.

With this book, I hope to change that. I am deeply grateful to the many grandfathers who were kind enough to share their stories and wisdom with me. I couldn't have done this without you.

This book isn't about any one person. It's about what we can do together for our grandkids. In partnership with our grandma mates, the change we can bring may be profound, with a whole new platform for turning all that is good about grandparents into something that will last for multiple generations, an evergreen library to better support our families.

Tom Brokaw—who I interviewed—has described the men and women of my parents' time as the greatest generation. They were indeed great. But I believe that our greatest generation is to come. The future leaders of the world are currently riding tricycles. They love *PAW Patrol* and Thomas the Tank Engine. A million paths lie ahead of them, and with our help they will navigate wisely.

Nurturing the next great generation is our purpose as grandpas, and I believe it is our obligation. We've seen how politics has torn America and other countries in two. We can get angry and write the usual fed-up Facebook posts. Or we can sit down with our grandchildren and teach them that just because a person has a different opinion doesn't make them bad. We can teach the importance of civility.

We can help our grandchildren reduce screen time. Put the phones away. And read book after book after book.

We can give our grown children advice, be there for them when they need us, and get out of the way when they don't.

We can learn from other grandparents and share wisdom to help us all do the best job we can at nurturing this next great generation. And we can have fun along the way, living our lives to the max.

I certainly don't have all the answers and never will. But what I can do is open a door to starting a discussion that can bring hope to a world that badly needs it. Our grandchildren deserve nothing less.

PROLOGUE

Fishing Down Between the Mountains

Simply saying the words "my father" in the opening sentence of this story gives away the happy ending, but this is the risk I have to take when telling you of the courtship of my mother, Janet, by the World War II US Navy lieutenant named Bill who would become my father. And the story of my grandfather, the Colonel, who believed—unreasonably—that no man was good enough for his daughter. That Janet had some say in who she married was true, but when facing my grandfather, even my strong-willed mother was surely put to the test.

Gramp, as I called him, was six foot three, a giant by the standards of the day, with sandy brown hair, a long, soulful face, and eyes and wit that sealed the deal for the ladies in his life. Gramp knew exactly what men were capable of, and by the time he'd joined the armed forces to fight the Nazis, his faith in *man*kind was at a low point when he learned that Janet and the lieutenant were serious.

Both Bill and Gramp were on leave at the family farm in the Northeast Kingdom of Vermont, staying at the farmhouse on the shores of Lake Willoughby—a place of such rugged beauty it deserves description as a central character in this book.

Five miles long and one mile wide, Lake Willoughby was formed when a glacier crawled down from Canada and gouged out the earth, forcing a mountain to give way at its center, tossing massive boulders aside in slow motion, and leaving behind a deep blue lake with sheer rock cliffs on either side. Eagles and hawks and ravens and seagulls and all manner of birds swoop and circle around the cliffs. When storms come in, the cliffs funnel the dark clouds and push them like boulders toward the line of red and white cabins that dot the shore. The surface of the lake is sometimes flat as glass, but more often it is a tumult of white caps.

The lake is deep, very deep, for the glacier that came through was intent on plowing up all in its path, burrowing down to yank every possible scrap of soil and rock up and out, up and out of the way. And when the thaw came, the water—bone cold to this day—filled the void. On a sunny day, you can look down into the depths and follow the light rays for a few feet, knowing that beyond your sight is a blackness that chooses not to give up its secrets. Hundreds of feet down it goes, to a place where trout the size of small horses lumber about in peace. Once in a while an ice fisherman in February hauls up some monster. You can see the photos pinned to the wall at the Willoughby general store. The fish are so big it's like they've been photoshopped. The fishermen clutch their catch and smile, part happy and part wondering in the back of their minds if they are holding something prehistoric—not really a trout at all—something that would eat them if they hadn't stuck the hook in first.

Go down between the mountains and no matter what kind of boat you're in, you can feel the deepness. It's like gravity. A force that is always there. We are guests on this part of the lake, skimming across its surface only by invitation of the deep waters, temporary and frivolous.

And it was here that Bill took Janet one day in August of 1943. He borrowed a forty-horsepower outboard motor from Gramp and attached it to the small wooden rowboat. Gramp had been cool to him all weekend, this young fellow who thought he was going to marry Janet. Yes, it's true my father was also tall. Yes, he was a fine-looking young fellow who served with the navy. Yes, the young man had seen combat. None of that meant he deserved Janet.

Janet was a fine catch. Five foot ten, with long brown hair and brown eyes and an oval face that lit up when she smiled. She was smart. She had a wit that could chisel granite. "Fun" didn't even begin to capture the sheer delight she showered all around her like rain glowing white in the sun. No wonder Bill fell for her. No wonder Gramp was not ready to give her up so easily.

Bill and Janet puttered out from the beach just down from the farmhouse and set a course for the southern end of the lake, the part faced by the twin rock cliffs.

The deep part.

It was a lovely summer day, but the waves were picking up with the growing wind as they hummed closer to the mountains. It took a good thirty minutes to get close to the cliffs, far from Gramp's disapproving eye. For Bill, this was not only a time to be with his true love. It was a time away from the war. A little bit of peace out there on Lake Willoughby, far from the horrors of battle.

He kissed her, she kissed him. They gazed into each other's eyes. And maybe at that moment Bill was reaching into his

My parents, Bill and Janet Page.

pocket to take out the ring; he was just about to shape his mouth into the words, "Janet, will you..."

...when suddenly the outboard motor fell off the back of the boat and disappeared. Bill stared in shock at the place where the motor used to be. Janet covered her mouth with her hand. "Oh no!"

"Damn," Bill said.

Gramp's motor was gone. And with it, Bill knew, went any chance of Gramp allowing his daughter to have anything to do with him. His marriage plans, you could say, were sunk. And not in just any piece of water. That motor had gone down in the deepest part of the lake, a place that laughs at you for trying to understand it.

US Navy Second Lieutenant Bill Page grabbed the oars. But before the first pull, he took note of the spot they were bobbing in and jotted in his memory the longitude and latitude of where the motor had dragged his hopes to the bottom.

Bill rowed for an hour to get back, against the wind. He said not a word, his jaw set, his eyes fiercely intent.

Janet cried.

Gramp was waiting on the shore. The fact that Bill was rowing, and the motor was no longer on the boat, was all Gramp needed to know. He stood there, glowering, as my tearful mother went to him with no words to say.

Bill trudged up to the garage, returning ten minutes later with a large bundle of rope and a grappling hook. And with only a dark look at Janet's silently judging father, he pushed off from shore.

You know of course—because I gave it all away in the first sentence—that Bill Page rowed through high waves down between the mountains, and under the rocky stare of the cliffs on either side of him, took note of his position, and lowered that grappling hook down, down, down, hundreds of feet of rope down, his entire future life dangling there, the life where he'd have five sons and many grandchildren, all of it so tenuous as to be completely hopeless to anyone but a man who loved Janet Fish so much he could not give up, and he got that grappling hook around that motor and hauled it up, the sun starting to go down and the wind rising higher and higher, and he hauled the motor like a giant fish into the bottom of the boat, and he rowed back with clenched teeth, and just as the dusk came to the sky with red and yellow streaks across the clouds he pulled the boat up onto the shore, exhausted, and went and found Janet and her father at the farmhouse.

When my father, grinning now, explained what he had done, Gramp laughed and clapped once. And then Gramp said something he'd never said before to any man who'd ever come near his daughter, the woman who would soon become Janet Fish Page, and eventually my wonderful mother. He smiled and patted Dad warmly on the back. "Well done," he said. "Well done."

In the fullness of time I, too, would catch my beautiful fish. We had two children, a girl and a boy, and they became fine adults. Not long after they graduated from college, they each married their high school sweethearts. And then, well, everything changed.

Find a comfortable chair—preferably one close to a deep lake—and I'll tell you the whole story.

CHAPTER 1

You're Boppy!

Today my daughter Abigail shared the news that I am
the grandfather of a heartbeat.
The ultrasound image was pasted into a Valentine's card
A black and white Rorschach with one tiny hand reaching up
as if to say, "Hello."
The boulder of energy that struck my chest was both kind
and playful.
It whispered of future walks in a Vermont meadow
Me holding my grandchild's hands up as she takes toddling steps
through the tall grass
His gleeful laughter at how new and thrilling it is to be alive
Smeared peas and Cheerios soggy with milk on a high-chair tray
And sitting together by the brook, staring in wonder and silence
At water spiders darting here and there.

—FEBRUARY 14, 2014

When my wife was due to give birth to our daughter, Abigail, we'd packed our bags for the hospital and were ready to go when the contractions started. I remember that feeling, the quickening of my heart, the excitement of heading into the experience as if it were a class IV white-water rapid, thinking I was ready but fearing I might not be—who could ever know?

This time, it was a call from Abigail that told me she was going into labor. I'd just had a relaxing glass of scotch and was watching TV. When I picked up the phone I expected a casual check-in call, but it was a different story. Abigail and her husband, Ryan, were at the hospital already. Contractions were steady. And because the baby was breech, there would be a C-section. In two hours. The rush of emotion and excitement all came back to me as if it were Abigail being born and not my grandson. I told Abigail I'd be driving down as soon as possible.

Nancy, at this time, was on a business trip, and I knew she'd be in a bit of a panic. I didn't want her to feel badly for not being there and was resolved to keep my calm and reassure her as well as my daughter that things were under control. Nothing, of course, is ever under control. When birth is involved, I knew from experience it was a joyous cavalcade of bodily fluids and wailing baby cries and slimy poop and the uncertainty of wondering if there would be the right number of fingers and toes and the billion other concerns that overwhelm even the best prepared mom, dad, or grandparent. You take a deep breath, keep moving, and hope to God things will work out.

I slept fitfully between texts from Ryan and Nancy. At 2:30 a.m. I received the text I had been hoping and praying for: Mother and baby are happy and healthy. His name was Henry Robinson Moore, taking my middle name. I sat on the edge of my bed and wept. *Thank you, God,* I said. *Thank you.*

I hit the road at 3:30 a.m. for New York City, guzzling hot coffee in the darkness and light rain on the Mass Pike, and arrived at NewYork-Presbyterian Hospital on the Upper East Side around 8:00. Abigail's hospital room was quiet when I entered, save for the tiny murmuring of a baby, my grandson.

The floor-to-ceiling hospital curtain surrounding Abigail's bed felt to me like the curtain in *The Wizard of Oz,* pulled back to reveal the old man feverishly tugging at levers, only now it was Abigail in the bed holding Henry, smiling up at me, Ryan grinning in a fatherly way beside them, and I was the old man.

Meeting your own child for the first time is amazing. Meeting your grandchild is similarly exhilarating, magical, and joyous. And yet there's something more to it, another layer. The hard work of raising Abigail right, nurturing and loving her, making sure she grew up in a nice town with great schools. Sending her to the college of her choice (George Washington, not coincidentally in the same city where Ryan—her high school sweetheart—was attending Georgetown). Celebrating her wedding on a beautiful old farm in Vermont with friends and family there to support her. All these things formed a kind of foundation for her life that she could then build upon. And even though I could not see all these things at that moment when I held Henry for the first time, I was aware of them and felt the love and effort of all that parenting as if it had been somehow condensed in time, right at the moment I saw this wonderful and handsome baby, Henry, my grandson. I held him in the crook of my arm and made no effort to stop the tears from streaming down my face. I whispered to him as much to myself, "Hi, Henry." He was so light and small. Deeply asleep. Content.

After I'd visited them for a while, I went back to Abigail's apartment on West 74th Street and slept for a few hours. When I called Abigail to say I was heading back to the hospital, she asked me to bring the diaper bag and the Boppy—a large horseshoe-shaped pillow women use when breastfeeding. Trekking across Central Park with a diaper bag and a Boppy is a singular experience that's hard for me to describe. Part of me felt like I was a new dad, like this was just—quite literally—another walk in the park for me. I saw young parents with kids in strollers along the meandering verdant walkways, and they cast knowing glances at me with my Boppy as if it was a totem of my fatherhood. I considered blurting out to strangers, "I'm not actually a new dad! The Boppy is for my grandson!" But I didn't. I reveled in the illusion instead.

When I arrived at the hospital room with the Boppy, Ryan and Abigail giggled at the sight of six-foot-six me holding it, with its multicolored illustrations of giraffes and elephants. Ryan looked thoughtful for a moment, then said, "Boppy. Maybe *you're* Boppy."

For months all my friends had asked me what I wanted my grandfather name to be. Grandpa? Pops? Gramps? I said I wasn't sure, and didn't know if it was actually up to me. When Ryan suggested that perhaps I was Boppy, it struck me that Henry and I had both been newly named at the same time. Both born into new lives, Henry launched into childhood, me ascending to newly minted grandfatherhood. I felt that my whole life was ahead of me.

That was ten years ago. What's become clearer with each passing year is that my whole life was actually ahead of me—not an entirely new life of course, but a very different one, so different that I am not the same guy I was before. In that long-ago life when I was a parent, small things could make me angry, my emotional trigger ready to fire at dumb things like bad drivers. Having time to hold a baby grandchild in the quiet of the night and hear nothing but the sound of our breathing put the petty annoyances of life in perspective. Reading my grandchildren the same books we used to read our children, like *Goodnight Moon* and *The Cat in the Hat,* felt like rediscovering magic. The often angry world still exists, but somehow I'm floating above it. I've been admitted to the best club in the world, one so exclusive no

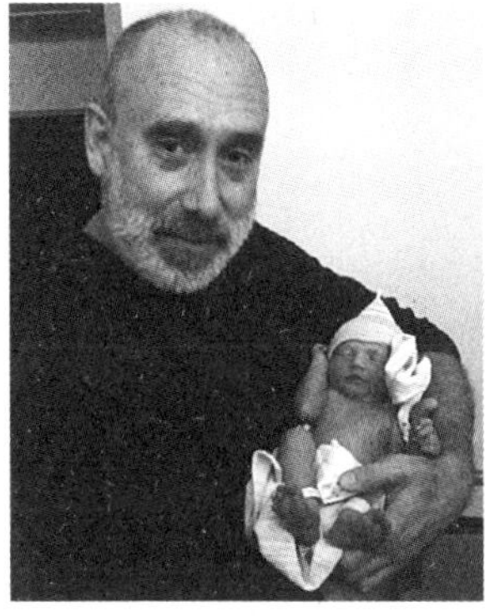

Holding my first grandson, Mr. Henry Robinson Moore.

amount of money can buy it. As you'll see when you read on, I've interviewed rich and famous grandpas, but most are regular Joes like me, and we are all on the same level playing field.

As Henry grew he was joined by a brother, then three cousins, all girls, and my name in time changed from Boppy to Grandpa Ted. They could call me anything and I'd be happy with it, because this is the new Ted, not the old Ted, which is ironic given that I'm getting older. I'm not alone in this sentiment. Many grandfathers become deeply changed for the better, as if we've emerged from a chrysalis to become something freer, lighter, happier. We are the ones who walk across Central Park with a smile on our faces, carrying within us a newly found contentment. We're the retired four-star generals sitting on the floor with their granddaughters playing with Barbies. We're putting on our reading glasses to help find the missing LEGO piece, and while we may have gray hair (or, in my case, no hair), we are boys again.

It's a new experience, yet it's not all new. There are still diapers. But we all have our roles to play in this new landscape. When I'm with one of our grandbabies and a particularly pungent aroma fills the room, I've been known to say to my son or daughter, while making my exit, "I think someone needs changing."

CHAPTER 2

Secrets of the Desk

Can an idea be an heirloom? I'm writing this book on the desk that belonged to my great-grandfather. When my father, William "Bill" Page, inherited it, he used it as his personal desk at home in his inner sanctum, an office on the top floor of our house outside Boston, the place where he did his deepest thinking.

As a kid I would sometimes sit at this desk and look at the note cards Dad had pinned on the wall. He'd created a compendium of wisdom gleaned from his voracious reading, one profound statement per card written in his neat all-capital lettering. The idea that stayed in my mind is a quote from George Washington Carver, the most prominent African American scientist of the early twentieth century: "Anything will give up its secrets if you love it enough."

I love this desk a lot, and in the course of time it has given up its greatest secrets, which I will share with you now. This matte-black nineteenth-century antique is solid as an icebreaker, with drawers painted inside in the particular red of British phone booths. Its lines are simple and angular, unadorned by flourishes. This is a desk for work.

Its family origins date back to the Civil War. My great-great-grandfather, Albert Kidder Page, served with a Massachusetts regiment. In July of 1863—the same month as the epic battle at Gettysburg—Albert was fighting his way through North Carolina when he contracted a severe case of malaria. When Albert's father, Luke, learned that his son was extremely ill, he traveled by train from Boston to retrieve him from the army hospital and bring him home. Albert's wife, Maria, was nine months pregnant. No doubt the family held out hope that Albert would recover and live to see his child born. But it was not to be. On July 3, Albert passed away in Maria's arms. Three days later, she gave birth to their son. She named him Albert Kidder Page (curiously, he was not a "Jr.").

Albert grew up, studied hard, and became a doctor. The desk was his. Boston, at the time, was a destination for Chinese immigrants, and Albert was one of the few doctors who would accept them as patients regardless of their ability to pay. He often accepted china in lieu of money. I'm guessing Dr. Page was right-handed, because there's a small spot on the top right of the desk where the paint is worn away due to repeated pressure from a writing instrument—his hand filling out prescriptions for all those in need of care. The china Dr. Page received from patients is still in the family, its value not measured in dollars.

Nearly one hundred years after the Civil War, when the desk was in my dad's office, he flew to California to attend a scientific conference. On his trip back to Boston an unknown woman approached him at the ticket counter at LAX and said, "Excuse me, I was wondering if you're on the earlier flight. It's urgent that I get home to my family, and I was hoping you'd consider switching flights with me." My dad was unfailingly kind and considerate of others, and he never seemed to be in a hurry, so it's no surprise to me that he agreed. She took his seat on the earlier TWA flight.

That plane collided with another over the Grand Canyon. All lives were lost. It was the worst civil air disaster that had ever occurred in the United States.

My dad arrived home safely and went back to work, continuing to read voraciously and write down new nuggets of wisdom to pin on the wall, including a new one: "Life is a gift." Whenever my dad told the story of the switched flights, he'd finish by saying, "And the moral of the story is, if someone asks you for a favor, do it!" I was born three years later. The only reason I'm here, and the reason why I've been able to get to know my grandkids, is because of chance and kindness. The gift of life that a total stranger gave my father—and by extension to me—must be somehow repaid.

Life went on. The desk was put to good use by my dad over the following decades, with countless letters written, scientific papers perused and annotated, wisdom captured. World peace was the underlying current of all my dad's thinking. Having lived through the horrors of Okinawa, he believed all war was incredibly stupid. The imperative for peace was infused into our family life in myriad ways, such as hosting exchange students. Building bridges of understanding with people from many countries would, in his view, create a more loving family of mankind. This is how a young student from Kenya came to live with us in the mid-1960s. His name was James Odhiambo.

While James spent time with us five boys—expanding our worldview in the process—it was really my dad who he bonded with the most. The full extent of that bond didn't become fully clear until recently. A month ago, one of my brothers discovered a letter written to my father from James's wife in 1983. In my mind's eye, I picture Dad opening the letter as he sat at this desk. Below is verbatim what she wrote:

> 12-10-83
>
> Mrs. Dinah Odhiambo
> P.O. Box 30101
> Nairobi, Kenya
>
> Dear Mr. Page,
>
> It is a really long time since you read from us and also read from you. I remember, the last time was, I sent you our family photo, you never mentioned whether it reached you or not.
>
> I thank God who has given me this chance to remember you. The [?] had come because of ups and downs, and thereafter, to give you a surprising news, I got my fifth baby. This one came after 7 years and I had not planned. God gave me a baby boy and my husband named him you, thus William-Page Odiwuor. Odiwuor means from midnight up to 3am and my baby arrived at 12:45am at night on 28-2-83. So, this means my husband together with me have not forgotten you. I have been troubled every now and then that I have you in our family, but I have never let you know. I don't know how you will take it, but my husband insisted we must name you in our family, and I think that is why I got this one after many years.
>
> I'm sure your wife is doing well together with the rest of the family. Please pass my warmest regards to all and may God bless you.
>
> Sincerely,
>
> Dinah Odhiambo

Later in the '80s we heard that James had died of AIDS. My dad likely sat here when he wrote a check to help pay for William-Page Odiwuor's college education. Since my dad was, like

James Odhiambo with my brothers, Charlie and Nick.

his grandfather, right-handed, the scratched paint on the desk was partly due to the tip of his pen bearing down as he wrote the check for young William, as Dad did for so many other people and the causes he cared about.

So, here I am today, working here at this old desk. It's not possible for me to write *Good Grandpa* and not think of those who wrote here before me. The prescriptions. The checks. The wisdom. Every fiber of this wood is imbued with the kindness of my ancestors and the gifts of strangers. I feel their presence as I sit here and type. I'm fortunate to know the secrets of this desk, passed down to me by spoken word and a letter found by chance. Through this book, the stories will be available to my children, my grandchildren, and hopefully everyone else. Heirlooms are nice things to receive. They are even better to give.

CHAPTER 3

The New Greatest Generation

It was an early morning in July 1918, cloudy with a strong wind blowing as the American pilot flew his Nieuport 28 biplane over Chamery, a hamlet of Coulonges-en-Tardenois not far from the front lines. His mission: Scout out and shoot down German reconnaissance. The fields of France were lush and green below, expanding out to the horizon where a glimmer of sun shone through the clouds, with dark trenches coiled through the fields like venomous snakes.

The roar of the engines behind him was his first sign of trouble; he turned with alarm to see three Fokker Chasse planes bearing down on him from above. He yanked the stick hard to maneuver and climb into a more favorable fighting position, hearing the rattling bursts of machine gun fire growing nearer. It was too late. Within seconds, he was shot twice in the back of the head. His plane turned over on its back and plunged to Earth.

Back home on Long Island, the young man's father—former president Theodore Roosevelt—mourned deeply. Roosevelt put on a brave face for the press, but many believed he was so heartbroken he never recovered. He died barely a year after his favorite son, Quentin.

In the same French skies that year was another American pilot. As he flew, he looked down at the battle below, a muddy moonscape of devastation, trenches separated by undulating piles and pits from shell blasts, shattered tree trunks pointing at twisted angles.

He pulled the trigger. But instead of firing a machine gun, he was snapping the shutter of a camera mounted to his plane to photograph German positions. He was smart. Resourceful. Brave. Lucky as hell.

He was my grandfather.

After the war, Fred Fish became a successful salesman and in middle age went back to Europe in World War II as a colonel.

I got to know Gramp very well, thankfully, when I was a teenager helping him and Gram maintain the rental cottages on our farm along the shores of Lake Willoughby.

Even then, in the 1970s, Gramp had a commanding presence. He'd fix me with his clear eyes and tell me to do this (empty buckets of sewage out of a septic well) or that (rake the beach). Or the Sisyphean task of cleaning the cottages using an upright vacuum that had terrible suction. I can picture him now as he kicked back at the end of a long day, drinking a Miller High Life in the yard behind the farmhouse.

Gramp lived into his mid-eighties, always active and full of life. He sang hymns in church, delighting everyone with his rich baritone. Often down at the beach he'd break into yet another chorus of his favorite song, "The Foggy Foggy Dew."

"You already sang that!" Gram would protest.

"Then I'll sing it again!"

Why does the fact that Gramp survived two world wars and lived a long life matter? Why did it matter to him, and—for the purposes of this book—why did it matter to me, my brothers, and cousins?

It turns out it matters a lot. Not just in the case of my Gramp, but for all grandpas and our loved ones here in America and around the world.

The reasons are rooted in the history of humanity itself. Early humans lived lives that Thomas Hobbes best described as "solitary, poor, nasty, brutish, and short."[1] Fossil records indicate that our very earliest ancestors thirty thousand years ago lived on average to about the age of thirty. Which meant very few lived long enough to become grandparents. Scientists aren't sure why Upper Paleolithic Europeans started to live longer into relatively old age, but they surmise that the changes brought about by this longevity had a profound impact on human evolution.

When more grandparents came on the scene, things started to change for the better. An article in *Scientific American* informs us that "grandparents contribute economic and social resources to their descendants, increasing both the number of offspring their children can have and the survivorship of their grandchildren."[2] In other words, having Grandpa and Grandma hanging out in the cave meant they were there to help raise the kids and dole out essential knowledge. Grandparents, for example, could teach how to plant seeds to get the best crops.

Gramp's habit of telling stories ladled with wisdom is likely a key reason why several of my four older brothers survived into adulthood. Here's one story out of many that shows how Gramp made a difference.

One Easter morning in 1969, we piled into the station wagon and headed over to our grandparents' house across town for our traditional feast of ham, potatoes, peas, pies, and handfuls

(Left) *My grandfather (Gramp) in World War I.* (Right) *Gramp's official WWI portrait.*

of chocolate Easter eggs. I was ten at the time, while my eldest brother, Calvin, was twenty-one, and Charlie nineteen. Both draft age for Vietnam. Photos taken that day seem inked in pastel hues, all of us in jackets and ties, young and pink-faced.

In some ways, life was normal, the war far away. But it was never far from our minds. Every night we watched Walter Cronkite on the evening news and saw body bags being loaded onto planes. My parents would watch the news with us and shake their heads. My dad had seen war close up and was no fan of it. Watching the Vietnam horror unfold on TV brought it all back for him.

Having seen Dad's PTSD up close, Calvin and Charlie were nervous about the draft; there was a lot of nail biting going on. Calvin was still a bit on the fence, though, about whether he'd volunteer. He'd been in ROTC in college and loved his guns. Charlie was more of a classic '60s hippy, complete with hair down to his shoulders.

(Above) *Gramp preparing for flight in France.* (Left) *Gramp as an air force colonel in WWII.*

That Easter, after we'd gorged ourselves on Gram's multi-course dinner, we retired to the living room. Somehow the topic of Vietnam came up. My grandparents—lifelong Republicans—had never said a word about Vietnam, which is why what Gramp told us that day was so memorable. He held court in his chair, center stage, while we sat nearby in respectful silence. "Well, boys," Gramp said, "when I went to war the first time, in World War I, they told us it was 'the war to end all wars.' Then came World War II, don't you know, and we had to go back and fight another one. Then there was Korea. And now there's Vietnam."

Here Gramp gestured one long hand for emphasis. "All I can tell you is, it's always the old men who start wars, and it's the young men who are sent off to fight them."

None of us said a word in response, but heads nodded. We knew exactly what Gramp's opinion of Vietnam was without him ever having to be explicit or betray his Republican principles. Charlie and Calvin chose not to volunteer and were not drafted.

Only a man who'd flown above the trenches in France, then returned to Europe to fight again had the moral credence required to make his message really sink in. My brothers and I lived on to have children and grandchildren of our own.

Benefiting from this intergenerational transfer of wisdom firsthand only made me want to know more about the role of grandpas in shaping the lives of young people. So I set out to meet with grandpas from all walks of life. What was the most essential wisdom they'd want to share? What stories might they tell that revealed a deeper truth? I wondered if I'd find one overarching commonality to their wisdom, or if what I learned would form a constellation of North Stars, each idea valuable in its own way but different. Maybe, I thought, what our grandchildren needed most was not one idea but rather some kind of playbook, a readily accessible compendium of wisdom gathered from our elders, the things we wished we'd known forty years ago.

* * *

WHERE TO START? Since my purpose was to nurture the next great generation, it made sense to begin with the man who wrote *The Greatest Generation,* Tom Brokaw. Tom and I had multiple exchanges via email where he kindly answered my questions about his life experiences and being a grandpa.

Tom was born in 1940 in the small town of Webster, South Dakota, the eldest of three brothers. His grandparents launched a hotel and meetinghouse that became a fixture of the town for decades, an enterprise that helped keep the family fed through the Great Depression. "My grandparents," Tom said, "were the 'can do' generation. Almost every chore required hands-on efforts. They were great role models, with little money, but their values were expressed through love, affection, and grandma's donuts!"

Tom's parents, Anthony Orville "Red" Brokaw and Eugenia "Jean" Conley, carried on the family traditions, always striving for a better life and working very hard to make it happen. Red became a skilled operator of earthmoving equipment and rarely if ever took a vacation. When Tom became the father of three girls, Grandpa Red didn't slow down; he just kept working hard and added a new job—delighting his grandchildren. "My kids were bedazzled by Grandpa Red's hands-on skills," Tom said. "One snowy Christmas we didn't have a sled, so he took his grandkids to his workshop and showed them how to make one out of spare lumber. It became the fastest sled on the hill."

Tom has modestly described himself as a lucky man, and while I'm sure luck played a role in his success, he no doubt worked his tail off to get ahead. Tom began his career with a small local news outlet, then quickly caught the attention of the big leagues. He became co-anchor of *The Today Show* in 1976 and went on to became anchor and managing editor of *NBC Nightly News*, a post he held for twenty-two years. Along the way, Tom won two Peabody Awards, two Emmys, the Presidential Medal of Freedom, and the French Legion of Honor. At the pinnacle of his career, Tom covered the fiftieth anniversary of D-Day in France, an experience that had a profound impact on him. Walking the beaches of Normandy with veterans of the Allied landing—the seminal event that ultimately led to the defeat of Nazi Germany—Tom came to see these men as something more, a cohort with humble roots who rose mightily to the occasion. In Tom's eyes, they were Americans who became great because that was simply what was required of them.

Tom's *The Greatest Generation* book ended up being more than just another bestseller. My baby-boom generation came to see our WWII-era parents as the gold standard for bravery and excellence in the face of adversity. If these extraordinary men and women were a precious metal forged through tough challenges, what kind of metal were we, their children? Personally, I always felt like copper or brass compared to my dad—nice for decorative effect, but not really cut out for doing what he did, like manning a radar station on a ship tossing in the Pacific as Japanese fighters buzzed overhead like dragons. The only dragons I've encountered were on HBO's *Game of Thrones,* and that suits me just fine. Today, I'm trying to figure out how our grandkids can become platinum, or some new and wonderous alloy. Beautiful and tougher than steel. Flexible and adaptive. And somehow kind and loving. So, I asked Tom if our grandchildren needed to face an existential threat in order to be forged into greatness.

"Tell them every day they'll encounter challenges," Tom replied. "And the test will be how they learn from each experience." When I probed deeper on this question, he added, "Every passage of time has an opportunity for knowledge. As the world becomes more crowded, mankind has an obligation to adapt to the changes—not just let the changes overwhelm us."

Viewed in this light, the challenges each generation faces may be unique to their time, but the qualities and behaviors needed to hurdle over the walls are the same: a combination of learning and positive resilience. We all fall down on occasion, but we're in the game. It's a concept Teddy Roosevelt famously championed in his 1910 "Citizenship in a Republic" speech...

> The credit belongs to the man who is actually in the arena, whose face is marred by dust and sweat and blood; who strives valiantly; who errs, who comes short again and again, because there is no effort without error and shortcoming; but who does actually strive to do the deeds; who knows the great enthusiasms, the great devotions; who spends himself in a worthy cause; who at the best knows in the end the triumph of high achievement, and who at the worst, if he fails, at least fails while daring greatly, so that his place shall never be with those cold and timid souls who neither know victory nor defeat.

Our grandkids are going to need this kind of grit. After all, they'll face their own existential threats. It would be nice to think they will sail through these storms without a scratch, but we know that's not likely to happen. AI is already making many jobs obsolete. Our grandkids may never be software coders, let alone Uber drivers. The environment continues to change for the worse, bringing more catastrophic floods and heat waves. Based on these challenges alone, it's likely our grandkids will be very much in the arena, boxing with every ounce of their strength.

At this point I asked Tom for the number one thing: What's the absolutely most essential wisdom that our grandkids will need in order to have a shot at becoming the greatest generation of all? He replied, "Life is not a key on autopilot. You have to earn every move."

At first I was a confused by this. "Tom," I wrote, "Did you mean 'earn' every move, or 'learn' every move?"

"EARN!" he replied (his all caps).

"What's an example of something we have to earn in life?"

"The affection of your kids," he said.

Honestly, it took me a while to digest that concept, but once I did it helped me see my life and relationships a little differently. My son and daughter are nearing forty, and I realize that I can never stop striving to earn their affection and trust. I will always be their dad first and foremost. Nor can I take my role as a grandpa for granted. Every move I make—whether that's helping out when the grandkids are sick, or getting down on the floor to help assemble annoyingly tiny LEGO pieces—is now part of my job. My résumé will be better for it.

A few months after my interview with Tom, one of my grandchildren experienced a trauma and was in a lot of pain. Ordinarily, I would have just done my usual routine to help out (retrieving ice packs from the freezer, and so on), but a subtle shift had begun in my mind. One of the most respected newsmen and authors of the twentieth century had shared *the* most important wisdom he'd learned his entire life. I couldn't just write about it; I had to use it. Isn't that what wisdom is for? So, while I applied the ice packs, I said, "I know this is hard. But it's important to remember that you're always going to have challenges like this in your life. What matters is how you learn from every experience. You're going to be OK."

My grandchild looked thoughtful for a moment, then a glimmer of a warm smile appeared, a slight lifting of the fear and gloom. "I know," he said.

CHAPTER 4

Flight of the Monarchs

The Tom Brokaw interview was just the beginning of my quest, and I suspected there was lots to learn from my own family—a challenge given that Gramp, along with my parents, had passed on.

This led me to seek out the advice of my oldest living relative, Aunt Lois, my mother's sister. Lois was ninety-five at the time, frail but sharp as a tack. In her long career Lois was a revered music teacher and an accomplished cellist. During World War II she became a pilot to help ferry mail across the United States. Like my mom, Lois had an acerbic wit. She and my mom would go for daily dunks in Lake Willoughby wearing matching bathing caps festooned with brightly colored rubber flowers. They'd chat while treading water.

The other thing Lois and my mom had in common was a deep love for their grandchildren. The grandpas I knew loved their grandkids just as much as the grandmas, but it was the grandmas who actually said so. Grandpas showed their love in other ways, like telling stories or simply doing chores with us (more on this in a later chapter).

Lois had six grandchildren and lived to enjoy her seven great-grandchildren as well. Surely, I thought, she could speak volumes about how I could be a good grandpa.

I caught up with Lois one day down at the family beach on Lake Willoughby. She was like a dry vine that had been bundled into a ball, arms and legs spindly, jaggy arthritic fingers twisted in odd directions. She could walk with a cane or with a loved one holding her arm, guiding her ship to dock with a thunk into the nearest chair. On the day I quizzed her, she was bundled in a sweater in the late August cool. She wore fabulous pink Jackie Onassis–style big-framed sunglasses.

"Lois, any advice on how I can be a good grandpa?" I asked.

Lois looked thoughtful for a moment, staring out at the lake and the waves swooshing onto the shore. Then she raised one bony finger and pronounced, "Be there for them!"

Me with my Aunt Lois down at the Lake Willoughby beach on the Fourth of July, 2017.

Setting the paper boats on fire.

Paper boats aflame at dusk.

I waited for her to continue. I figured her statement was merely a preamble to a longer, more eloquent oration. But no, that was it. And the more I thought about it, the more I knew she was right. If she had spoken for a whole day, or a year, she could not have imparted better advice. Abraham Lincoln's Gettysburg Address was among his briefest speeches but by far the most famous. Yet Lincoln's address, at 272 words, was positively verbose by Lois's standards. Great ideas are a lot like acorns. All the DNA of the tree is there. When planted and nourished, the acorn thrives into a massive oak tree. In the case of what Lois had told me, that tree had sprawling branches that hugged and protected all those she loved most.

Lois lived those words. Even up until the last year of her long life, when any movement at all caused her pain, she'd be there for us and her many grandchildren and great-grandchildren. Every year on the Fourth of July, Lois was the "boat lady" for our annual celebrations at the beach. Around dusk the wind would die down and leave the lake flat as a mirror, and in its reflection the roses of dusk bloomed as the sun slowly set. We'd light the bonfire as the whole family gathered around, talking and laughing, and Lois would sit at the picnic table and teach our bustling kids how to fold newspapers into paper boats.

Just as the sun was leaving the sky and the stars began to peek out, adults helped the kids put a match to their boats and launch them onto the water; the shimmering flames of a dozen ships floated slowly out onto the lake, the kids cheering theirs on; the winner would be the last boat still burning.

In her younger days, Lois would stand on the dock and play taps on her bugle. At ninety-five, she sat in her chair and sang along with us around the bonfire, withered with time but still a young mother inside.

In 2021 Lois passed away quietly in bed. The night before she died, she excitedly told my cousins that she had a busy day ahead of her. She was going to see Ray (her late husband), her sister, mother, and father. There was so much to look forward to.

This summer and for all summers to come, the paper boats will still flame and glitter along the shores of the lake at dusk. There's some of Lois in every fold of those boats and in every squeal of excitement as the kids set their boats aflame and watch them float and sputter.

It makes me very happy to know that Lois provided me with this sage advice, and to realize—through my discussions with dozens of grandparents—that there are as many ways to be there for grandkids as there are leaves in a forest.

* * *

My dad, Bill Page (Grandpa Bill to my children), had his own way of being there for me and my kids, one that was outside the mainstream—to put it mildly. Since my dad is a recurring character in this book, I'll paint a more complete portrait of him here so you can fully appreciate his delightful eccentricities.

Born in 1922, Dad was a child of the Great Depression. His father, my grandfather Roland, died of tuberculosis when Dad was only seven. Which meant that not only did Dad not have any grandfathers in his life, he also lacked a father to guide him. Or one that could provide for his family. His mother, my grandmother Margaret, worked as a secretary and struggled to keep food on the table when things got rough. Dad persevered, studied hard, and put his deep intelligence to work throughout his school years. He was accepted by Harvard but there was no money for tuition, so he took a full-ride scholarship to Tufts.

My dad was six foot three, with Gregory Peck looks—handsome, and well dressed in gray flannel suits. His brown eyes had a thoughtful sparkle, giving me the sense that a deep river was always running through his mind. Because it was. Large eyebrows arched over his eyes like the wings of a hawk, which in his grandpa years turned seagull white.

Dad earned his master's in chemical engineering from MIT. Then, on the eve of World War II, he took classes at Harvard to learn how to operate a new technology called radar; this eventually led to him serving as a US Navy radar officer in the Pacific Theater. He was one of the rare veterans who felt a deep sense of guilt over the atomic bombings of Hiroshima and Nagasaki. Oppenheimer was not alone.

My dad in the US Navy, WWII.

Questioning the status quo was so central to his parenting style that he literally stuck the word "why" in our faces every day. He wrote the word (all caps with an exclamation point: WHY!) on note cards that he taped to our bathroom mirrors. It wasn't a question; it was a command.

When my friends' dads took them out in the yard to play catch, my dad would take me on nature walks in a meadow. He'd unpack the antique brass microscope that used to belong to his father, and we'd slip a tiny speck of lichen between the glass to examine it. Why, he asked, did lichen survive through the harshest winters? Why did every piece of lichen look different, yet always beautiful? WHY! When I was exhausted from all the questioning and wishing I was back home watching TV, he'd say, "As you get older, you must never lose your capacity for wonder." As a father and a grandpa, my dad intertwined this lifelong sense of wonder with his passion for science. And he understood full well that doing activities with his grandkids would inculcate this passion far better than a mere lecture.

Here's just one Grandpa Bill story out of many that illustrates his wily ways. One day when I was at my parents' Vermont home on vacation, Dad decided to conduct an experiment with my kids, Abigail (then twelve) and Nicholas (nine). My mom had killed two mice and was going to toss their furry corpses into the woods. Dad retrieved the mice in the nick of time and stapled them onto a foam-core board, arms and legs splayed out. He brought my kids outside to show them this macabre display and asked, "How did the mice die?" My kids were a bit stunned, turning their palms up.

"Do you want to find out?" Dad asked.

"Sure!"

Dad handed them each a scalpel and instructed them on how to do a forensic autopsy. My delighted kids went to work. They soon cut open the mouse stomachs to discover they were full of little pink poison pellets. Eureka! Case solved.

My daughter credits this experience as inspiration for her getting a master's in communication science. Today, she's a speech pathologist teaching children with learning disabilities. Her students adore her, and she's making a real difference in their lives. My son became a successful graphic designer for a top corporation, and while art is his milieu, his work is imbued with a scientific curiosity that brings it to original places.

Most of us grandpas are not likely to create a CSI Vermont crime lab with our grandkids, but I've learned there is no right or wrong way to be there for them. It's the variety that adds up to something remarkable, including everyday activities that may at first seem ordinary. The story of Buck Weaver provides a good example, a story that begins with the migratory phenomenon of the monarch butterfly.

The monarch earned its regal name thanks to its brilliant orange-red wings, with black veins and white spots along the edges, forming royal robes that flutter through the air. At summer's end each year, millions of monarchs begin a three-thousand-mile journey south from New England to their winter home in the mountains of central Mexico, an area of forest comprising less than five acres.

The monarchs that take flight in northern Vermont, however, are not the same ones that will arrive in Mexico, because it requires multiple generations of them to fly, feed, and reproduce over such a great distance. Those I see from my front porch will carry the genetic torch only part of the way. Their offspring will take it from there, again and again and again. Scientists know them as *Danaus plexippus,* which is Greek for "sleepy transformation." They pollinate plants along their journey and stop—like weary highway travelers—at monarch way stations where they lay their eggs on the undersides of milkweed leaves. Their progeny undergo a magical metamorphosis, crawling free as caterpillars, then forming into light-green chrysalises before finally spreading their lustrous wings to take flight.

One such monarch way station is the island of Key West, in southern Florida, where Buck Weaver and his wife live in the winter months. Buck, a retired orthodontist, is a boyish seventy-eight with sandy whitish-blond hair and boundless energy. He and his wife have three kids and an eight-year-old grandson, Felix.

When Buck was a young boy, living for a time in Hawaii when his dad was stationed there, he developed a fascination with the caterpillars that thrived on the island. Many decades later—once again living on an island—Buck rediscovered his love of caterpillars and their transformational wonders.

"So, literally a few days ago, I had a palm frond that had six chrysalises on it," Buck told me excitedly when we met on Zoom. "When they come out of the chrysalis the wings are all folded up of course, the abdomen is unbelievably fat, and literally in the first two to three minutes they pump all the fluid out of the abdomen into the wings. If you look at the little stripes on the wings, those are the veins—literally like tissue paper. They can't fly. And they have to sit there for two hours. So, the point of my story is, when my grandson visits, he's up every day checking on the caterpillars."

Buck is there for Felix to spot caterpillars hidden under leaves, then patiently observe their metamorphosis into monarchs. When they're not examining butterflies, they're swimming in the azure sea. "Felix spends hours and hours and hours with his mask and snorkel," Buck said. "Off course I've been with him. We see mangrove, snappers, and grunts and other species. He can name the fish."

When I asked Buck for his number one piece of wisdom, he didn't skip a beat. "Be nice to people!" But in the very same breath he added, "It's monarchs and the love of nature. To be out in nature and have an appreciation of it." For Buck, the concept of being nice embraced being kind and respectful to all the living things around us. I knew this with certainty when Buck finished telling me his story about the monarchs. He had observed a butterfly that, upon emerging from its chrysalis, had dropped to the ground and bent its wing. "If you can catch it in the first few minutes—before the wing begins to harden—you can straighten it out and get them back up on a leaf," Buck said. He did a quick repair to improve the monarch's chances of making it home. "You know," he continued, "in nature one out of ten thousand make it. I like to think I can make it five or six out of the ten thousand."

Before we finished our conversation, Buck looked wistful and said, "I'm thinking about teaching grandkids to love what you love. I would hope that twenty years from now my grandson will be diving, but if he's not, that's OK. If he were to take his own kids to an aquarium he'll say, 'I used to look at fish with my grandpa.' Which is pretty cool for his own kids."

Yes, I thought, very cool indeed.

The paper boats aflame at dusk on the waters of Lake Willoughby, the "aha" moment of the mouse autopsy, and the lifelong sense of wonder at monarch metamorphosis have a common thread that forms a pattern. We don't actually "spend" time with grandkids. We can't spend what we never owned to begin with, because the time we have on this Earth is merely a gift that we are holding on to for a while. What we're really doing is creating and sharing experiences, and we do this by following the sage advice of Joseph Campbell—*follow your bliss.* Campbell, who authored books such *The Hero with a Thousand Faces,* made a lifelong study of ancient mythologies and the wisdom we can glean from them. George Lucas credited Campbell's work as inspiration for his *Star Wars* films.

For my aunt Lois, teaching her great-grandchildren how to fold paper boats was pure bliss. Red Brokaw loved working with his hands, so he put Tom's kids to work building a sled from scratch. My dad's love for science turned into an unforgettable lesson in discovery for my kids. Buck's fascination with nature—acquired when he himself was a child—is a blissful heirloom he's passing on to young Felix. Individually, these experiences are wonderful. But imagine millions of grandparents all over the world following their bliss in myriad ways. My God, what a difference it makes, what a beautiful vision, a coruscation of monarchs fluttering across the Gulf of Mexico.

As fate would have it, just as I was working on this chapter my wife and I were enlisted to babysit our two granddaughters. My son and his wife had planned a much-needed getaway to a spa, and we were more than happy to help out. Babysitting was a timely reminder that we need to also be there for our grown kids, these hardworking parents, as much as our grandkids.

Truthfully, as any parent can attest, babysitting is not always a bucket of bliss. When we slept over at our son's house to babysit, our youngest granddaughter, Mae, woke up at least once every hour all night long with loud cries of "I'm scared!" or "I want Grandma!" or "I want my water bottle!" By 4:00 a.m. I was completely exhausted and recalled—not for the first time—that sleep deprivation is a common torture technique. I think I finally fell asleep around 5:00 a.m. and shortly thereafter was woken up by our five-year-old granddaughter standing beside the bed pleading, "When are you going to wake up?!"

I spent much of the morning guzzling coffee and trying not to be irritable. Still, all in all, that sleepless night was precious to me because it was a lesson I needed to relearn. Being a parent is tough. It's exhausting. Our kids need our support, and they will always need our support. We have to remember that the monarchs flying home to Mexico are three or four generations removed from their ancestors up north. Each generation nurtures the next. We grandparents help to create a restful way station for our kids that allows them to continue on. We are the underside of the milkweed where they can sleep and dream. We're not just about fun and games. We have a purpose. We will get weary along the way, but the energy to do the right thing is within us all. As Obi-Wan Kenobi would say, "Feel the Force!"

CHAPTER 5

Labors of Love

As my wife and I have settled into our grandparenting experience, I've often wondered about the different roles played by grandpas and grandmas, and how those differences may have changed since the time I knew my grandparents.

I can only remember my Gramp as part of an inseparable pair with my Gram, who was a force of nature. She was petite but with a giant presence, and indefatigable in her work on the farm and cottages. When Gramp was in England serving in World War II, Gram was a national leader in the Girl Scouts; she wore her uniform just as smartly as Gramp wore his. Gram and Gramp both worked hard, just at different things (he did chores like carpentry and plumbing, she cooked and cleaned and mended clothes). The biggest difference I can observe now over the distance of time is how they expressed their love. Whenever we had family picnics, Gram would share a poem she'd written and before ending her oration say things like, "Most of all, I'm grateful for our grandchildren, who I love dearly." Gramp would observe this with a smile, sipping his Miller, but not add his own words of adoration. His way of showing affection was to put us to work.

My mom was a hugger. My dad, not so much. Mom would often smile and wink at me and say, "I love ya, kiddo!" I can't recall my dad ever saying anything like this when I was growing up. This male/female difference, however, is by no means universal. My wife recounts that her dad, Pat, would tuck her and her sister into bed each night and tell them, "Daddy loves you." But, by and large, for most of the men I've spoken with, doing hard work together was how their fathers and grandfathers showed affection.

To illustrate this, I'll bring you back with me to a summer day in Vermont in the early 1970s when I was thirteen and deep into reading J. R. R. Tolkien's *The Lord of the Rings*. Just as my mind was fully enmeshed in Middle Earth, my dad came up to my bunk and asked, "Hey, Ted, how would you like to build a hobbit-hole?"

"What?"

"We'll build a hobbit-hole, up in the field. I've got the plans all drawn up."

"Sure!" I said.

For three summers in a row my brothers and I sweated and toiled with shovels, pickaxes, and wheelbarrows to dig our hobbit-hole—an underground house—at the edge of our field. First, Dad had a backhoe dig out an indentation in the ground that formed a dome, its peak level with the field. He had workers place steel reinforcing rods over the dirt dome, then pour concrete over the rods to form what would become a three-foot-thick, steel-reinforced roof. Before the backhoe pushed dirt over the dome, he stapled photos of Hiroshima burn victims to foam-core boards and put them face down on the concrete. His quasi-mystical conception of chemistry led him to believe that the photos would emanate thoughts of peace downward into the hobbit-hole, making it a peace dome. Anyone inside would be able to focus on ways to bring about world peace.

Once the dirt was pushed over the whole thing, the backhoe left. It was not lost on us that the heavy machinery was sent on its way before the hobbit-hole was actually dug. The backhoe was only there to fashion the domed roof. Our job was then to dig under the dome from the edge of the field, by hand, to create the solitary room that would comprise the hobbit-hole.

It was incredibly strenuous work. Picture teenagers pushing loaded wheelbarrows out of an underground structure up a steep incline, screaming with the effort, muscles straining, gritted teeth, dozens of times in a day over three long summers. Dad was right there with us. His digging outfit was always the same—khaki shorts and a white T-shirt, all filthy and drenched with sweat. We built up the concrete walls of the hobbit-hole in stages as we removed more dirt, so the circle of blocks grew the more we dug. My brother Nick and I learned that the acoustics underground, surrounded on all sides by concrete, were fantastic for close vocal harmony. We'd take breaks to sing "Swing Low, Sweet Chariot" and other songs, basking in the cool dimness with the lush sounds reverberating all around us.

Did my dad engineer a steel-reinforced concrete roof because we were making a nuclear bomb shelter? Perhaps, but what were the chances of a Russian missile going wildly off course and hitting a remote northeast corner of Vermont? Did he make us do hard labor to toughen us up? I doubt it. This was many years before teenagers lounged around the house playing video games. We were already outside working to maintain the cottages, and when we weren't working we were climbing mountains or swimming. Was my dad so traumatized by his

World War II PTSD that he forgot fundamental principles of engineering and design? Again, not likely. He was in the prime of his career at Polaroid.

Back then, these questions barely occurred to me. I just thought the hobbit-hole project was a gas. And besides, none of my friends had a hobbit-hole, so I had bragging rights. (I'm still bragging about it!)

Only in hindsight today, as a grandfather, can I see the exquisite method in my dad's madness. With every wheelbarrow of dirt I hauled out of the ground, with every new cinder block stacked in the growing circular wall under the peace dome, Dad was saying, "I love you." Years later when my children were growing up, Dad would often put them to work with him to haul brush, in the rain.

My Gramp would not be outdone in the Labor of Love category. He must have loved me a lot, because he worked me like a dog. The hard toil that made the biggest impression on me took

Me, Dad, and my brother John at the entrance to the hobbit-hole about ten years after the digging.

place one late summer morning up at the lake, the maple leaves still green but here and there painted red and yellow from a few frosty nights. I thought I'd gotten away with having a day off from farm chores, not to mention the hobbit-hole, but Gramp tracked me down.

"Teddy! I have a job for you," Gramp said, handing me a heavy six-foot-long crowbar. "Follow me." As always, he was dressed head to toe in khaki, bent forward at the waist and walking with his hands clasped behind his back. It was around eight in the morning. I dreaded having to do another chore, but there was no saying no to Gramp. Even a whimper of discontent could provoke a silent glare that would crush my preteen soul. Gramp instructed me to carry the crowbar into the brook that runs through the farm, a gurgling ribbon of water that runs down from Westmore Mountain into Lake Willoughby. It's called Myers Brook, named for my great-grandmother who owned the farm in 1908.

My feet, in old Keds sneakers, became icy cold in seconds as I stood in the brook and looked up at Gramp, wondering what was needed of me.

"OK, Teddy, now I want you to move that rock there over to the side. You'll have to get the bar under it to pry it loose."

I looked at the rock he was pointing to, an intimidating boulder. It took a few tries and a lot of digging to pry it loose from the sand, but after much grunting and pushing I managed to move it a few feet to the side where Gramp wanted it.

"That's just dandy," he said. "We're almost done. Now, see that rock over there? I want you to move that one over to here."

The rock he was pointing to looked like it was from Stonehenge, but I did as I was told. As the hours wore on I began to sweat more and more, which attracted swarms of blackflies like honey for bears. My ankles were getting scraped and bloodied by the rocks.

"Oh, that's a big one, isn't it, Teddy! Now move that one there..."

"This one?"

"Yes, move that one over to here, and we'll be almost done!"

Many hours later I was tired, banged up, and bruised, and Gramp was still there, indefatigable, towering over the brook, pointing at this rock and that rock. It wasn't until late afternoon that Gramp paused. "That's just dandy," he said. "Wonderful."

I stood there breathing hard, a tall, sagging, limp rag of sweat and black fly bites, and surveyed the newly rocky banks of the brook. Winter is never far away in northern Vermont. The heavy snows would come soon enough, followed in time by a great melting that would send mountain water cascading down in a roar, but I knew that these sturdy banks would hold without erosion, our family's land preserved for another year.

Gramp took the crowbar from me and smiled. He said when walking away, as much to himself as me, "There's no substitute for hard work."

* * *

ON A RECENT JULY FOURTH WEEKEND, my grandkids joined their cousins down at the beach to prepare for the big bonfire and the lighting of the paper boats. We grown-ups hauled armfuls of dry brush from the forest and tossed them onto the tip of land close to the water where the bonfire would be, near the edge of Myers Brook. Our children—now in their thirties—instructed our grandchildren to carry driftwood from the edge of the water and put it on the bonfire. All of them eight or younger, the littlest barely one, they carried the heaviest pieces of wood they could manage. One stick, then another, and another. Small sticks added on by degrees to grow a larger and larger pile of brush. Adults threw on logs. At one point a grandchild complained he was tired. "We're not done," my daughter told him gently but firmly, and he continued on without further complaint. In time, a fine pile of wood was heaped by the shore.

Our intergenerational labor of love bore fruit when the bonfire was lit. The very smallest and thinnest twigs, the ones carried there by the toddlers, went up in flames first to ignite the larger sticks and logs, and soon the fire grew and grew and painted our faces with a warm reddish glow.

When I think back on my time moving boulders in the brook, I realize that learning how to work hard without complaint was only one piece of a larger puzzle. Gramp pushed me to not only move the boulders, but to arrange them perfectly against the banks so the rocks fit tightly together as any stone wall should. The larger the gap between the stones, the more likely erosion would occur. Robert Frost could not have fashioned a nicer stone wall, and the ones I had to build were at an angle, sloped just so, leaving a bed below for water to flow with abandon. Doing the job right was the only way to do it.

There have been many times in my adult life when I have stood on the bridge that spans Myers Brook and gazed at the water below. You can learn a lot about writing by staring at a brook. The water flowing is an idea, and when it comes to a rock it curves around without stopping, a kind of physical comma, and semicolons are the larger rocks that temporarily obstruct more of the water flow; they don't fully stop the water but interrupt it just long enough to enunciate one flavor of the larger idea and add another closely related idea, and water continues to flow into small pools where thoughts can intermingle with others, the eddies invisible but for the extra effort of water spiders desiring to hold in place, or leaves on the surface slowly circling, and on the water rushes faster and unimpeded through narrow channels of stone, and only when the idea has fully run its course into the lake there's a period of sorts. Writing a well-crafted paragraph is hard work, but I know—even at the very outset—that I am almost done.

I see these flowing stony brooks of thought in the work of writers like Norman Maclean. The last pages of his *A River Runs Through It* are particularly masterful and leave me breathless because I'm right back on the bridge looking at the water flowing, remembering Gramp, and seeing the rocks where they need to be.

As our grandkids grow up in a world where "smart" phones are a constant distraction, I hope I will be indulged when I ask them to turn them off and come with me to look at the brook. Just look, nothing else. They might ask, "Why?"

"Well," I'll reply, "that's an excellent question. I'll tell you a story."

CHAPTER 6

The Call of Nature

Grandpa Bill experienced the woods as a kind of church. The soaring birch and maple trees arching over his path formed the spires of a cathedral, the deep green moss and ferns beneath were holy velvet, the gurgle of water sprouting down the brooks were hushed conversations on weighty matters, the hoofprints of deer a sure sign that he was on the right track toward his version of God. He encouraged his many grandchildren to follow his example, to stop and listen to nature, because only nature could tell you everything you needed to know.

This was the man, who, at the age of seventy-five, decided one crisp fall day to hike Wheeler Mountain, near Lake Willoughby. In a land of craggy mountains, Wheeler is especially rocky and not a place for anyone afraid of heights. At its base, the trail flows up through a stand of sapling maples, but soon a hiker is confronted by cliffs. The white trail markers on trees are replaced by faint and infrequent smudges of white on boulders. Wet moss often spans across stretches of rock, making the trail a challenge for twenty-five-year-olds and grandfathers alike.

Dad in nature, his church.

After an hour or so of near vertical ascent, the intrepid hiker is rewarded with a long expanse of open rock above the tree line, with only short evergreens here and there clinging to small pockets of earth.

And it was here along this ridge that my dad hiked by himself, filling his lungs with fresh-smelling air, seeing below the broad, undulating valley in peak foliage, and a few miles to the east the five-mile stretch of the lake bracketed at its southern edge by Mounts Pisgah and Hor.

No doubt Grandpa Bill was wearing his customary fall outfit of khaki shorts and red-checkered flannel shirt. He paused atop an outcropping of rock along a cliff near the summit, a kind of pulpit, and suddenly, as he put it, "felt the call of nature" and unleashed a high yellow arc of pee that projected out and down. He followed the arc as it splashed against a rock forty feet below.

The rock began to move.

Always attuned, as I've said, to the wonders of nature, Grandpa Bill was quite surprised and not a little baffled that a mere stream of piss would make a boulder move, but when the rock stood up the realization that it was a black bear—a really angry black bear—gave him a tremendous jolt.

A casual observer, perhaps an owl perched in a nearby tree, would have been hard-pressed to determine who was more surprised, the bear being splashed by this red-checkered demon above, or my dad, whose hair stood up and turned whiter.

The growling bear, quite literally pissed, started up the cliff toward him.

Grandpa Bill ran. After a minute he turned his head to see if he was in the clear, but the bear was still coming his way, and getting closer. I suspect at this point that my dad set a land speed record for his age group as he raced down the mountain, not thinking to zip up his pants until he arrived, safely, back home.

My dad told this story often, making his grandchildren peel with laughter until their sides hurt. It was funny of course, but there was also wisdom embedded in the tale. First, be very careful where you pee. And most important, be sure to stay in shape when you get older; you never know when you'll need to sprint.

CHAPTER 7

Unsilly Wisdom from John Cleese

Getting older and wiser allows one to gain some perspective on humor and life itself. This made me think of another grandpa I know, a fellow who's learned a few things about how funny life can be. John Cleese came to mind, especially because I've written various projects with him as the star.

On the first video I did with John, he was cast as several characters in my script for *The Institute for Backup Trauma,* a viral marketing project for a client that had a new and more reliable product for data backup. John played the head of the institute, which catered to people who had lost their minds after losing their data. Being a ham myself, I made sure I wrote myself a cameo so I could appear briefly on camera with the man I revere as my comedy God. In addition to playing the role of Dr. Harold Twainweck, John gamely wore a dress and curly wig to play the role of Hilda, an office manager at the Toothy Grins dental supply company. My script described Hilda as buxom to the point of disability. In his trailer dressing room, John tried on

Me with John Cleese (Hilda) in The Institute for Backup Trauma.

numerous outfits for the Hilda character until he finally put on a tight red sweater over his prodigious bust, at which point he looked into the mirror and said purringly, "I just feel sexy." John carried it well, and still managed to keep his mustache, lending him the appearance of an elderly cross-dresser who Ron DeSantis would have banned from Disney World.

John has played many roles since the time he worked with me, including that of Nearly Headless Nick, one of the Hogwarts ghosts in *Harry Potter*. But these days John also plays the role of grandfather, presumably managing to keep his head on. I met up with him over lunch recently when he was in town to do a show, joined by my friend Doug. This was not a formal interview by any means, but rather a sprawling two-hour lunch conversation. I've been a fan of John's work since his early days with Monty Python, so it was a real treat to kick back, have a good meal, and get caught up. John doesn't like to dwell too much on the Pythons, but inevitably a few tidbit remembrances of those days were served up, such as the crafting of the "Parrot Sketch." Apparently, John and his main writing partner, Graham Chapman, knew that the dead animal returned to the pet shop could not be a dog or cat because people are rather fond of them, but everyone hates parrots.

In the course of our conversation, I mentioned that I was writing a book and hunting for elders who could share the number one thing, the most essential wisdom, to offer the next generation.

John immediately jumped in. "It's very simple," he said, "because I'm reading about this all the time: 'It's more important to *find out* what's right than to *know* you're right.'"

When I pressed him to unpack this idea, he explained that for two hundred years everyone believed that Newton's laws of physics were the last word; then Einstein came along with the theory of relativity, and the old assumptions went out the window. Then quantum physics upended even Einstein's beliefs. The mindset of assuming one knows the truth can be highly detrimental, whereas seeking to find the truth—which can be a long, fascinating, beautiful journey—is what really matters.

I love this idea, and I'm glad I had a chance to talk with John in the early stages of my learning quest. At no point can I truly believe I know the answer. The magic will be in traveling to find it.

John Cleese may be a comedic lion in winter—his eighty-five-year-old legs long past the silly walks stage—but he's just as funny as ever. His show the night of our lunch was billed as "An Evening with the *Late* John Cleese." I laughed uproariously, gleefully, endlessly, a grandpa who felt seventeen again. I left my Cleese reunion refreshed and ready to gallop into the unknown.

CHAPTER 8

The Fuel

On August 14, 1936, rowing crews from six countries competed for the gold medal at the Olympic games in Berlin, Germany. Adolf Hitler was in the stands, cheering on his team at the Grünau Regatta Course. There were eight rowers and one coxswain per boat on the two-thousand-meter race, one oar per rower, with a photo finish that became legend as the American team took home the gold. The story of the team's journey from their humble origins in Washington state to becoming heroes is brilliantly told by Daniel James Brown in *The Boys in the Boat* and in the movie adaptation directed by George Clooney.

But there is another story here that's important to tell. One that spans generations that lived before 1936, and after, and will extend into the future.

The nine American rowers in the boat that day had an extra teammate, an alternate ready to replace anyone injured or ill prior to competition. His name was Delos "Dutch" Schoch. According to family lore, at one point when Dutch was filming the team, he was blocking Hitler's view and was summarily asked to move. When I learned this it made me wish a lot more people had stood in Hitler's way in 1936.

After serving in the navy in World War II, Dutch became head rowing coach at Princeton University. His love of rowing was passed on to his son, Fred Schoch, who played a leading role in building one of the great sports competitions in the world today, the Head of the Charles Regatta, held yearly in Cambridge, Massachusetts.

When I heard a little about Fred's storied family life—and learned he has four grandkids—I knew I had to meet up with him over coffee. (In the course of writing the book, I've turned my local Starbucks into a virtual conference center for grandfather networking.) When I have these conversations I wear big ears, asking lots of questions and trying to stay open to where the story leads me. With Fred, I was curious about how his upbringing influenced him, and how those influences in turn guided him as a father and today as a grandfather.

The first thing I discovered was that Fred Schoch is easy to spot in a coffee shop. He has a large, athletic frame, making the round table before him seem miniature, and he has a mop of white hair.

While Fred's grandfathers passed away before he had a chance to know them, it was clear from the outset of our conversation that his father—and the love of rowing—had a big influence on him.

"My dad was this heroic Hemingwayesque figure," Fred said. "Big as I am, burly. A revered coach. He was a man of few words, but when he spoke you really paid attention."

Fred grew up in the 1950s in Princeton, New Jersey, at the time a sleepy little town. Fred believed he was shaped by not only his father, but the impressive young oarsmen who rowed for Princeton University. When he was a very young boy, the team playfully threw him into the bus luggage rack and took him along on trips. He started with the team as a coxswain when he was only ten years old, over time joined the team's workouts, and eventually rowed with them. In 1960, he steered one of his father's crews in the 1960 Olympic trials in Syracuse, New York.

One of Fred's fondest memories of his dad was on wintery Sunday afternoons. They lived on fifteen wooded acres lush with oak trees, and they had a fire going all winter in their prerevolutionary farmhouse. Dutch would take Fred out in an open Willys Jeep deep into the woods to cut up the wood of fallen trees with a heavy Sears, Roebuck chain saw. "So, I learned how to split logs," Fred said, "and actually wrote a poem to my son, Willard, about that experience and I gave it to him for his birthday about ten years ago. Your relationship with your kids is so important. I took my youngest son to the airport recently and he said, 'Dad, I'm really glad you gave me a ride because it's more than that. It's symbolic. I want you to know how important you are and how much I want you to be in my life.'"

Fred's own father died from a coronary at the age of fifty-six. "You begin to think about the uncertainty of our lives when you hit seventy," Fred said with a wistful smile. "The lights can go out at any time." Fully mindful of life's brevity, Fred made a commitment to retire from the regatta so he could spend more time with his grandkids.

As Fred talked, I heard echoes of my own experiences: the quiet bonding when tackling hard work, the simple act of being there for his grandkids. In Fred's case, given his background, I wondered out loud what lessons he hoped to impart when he spent more time with his growing team of offspring.

"I think it's important to pass on the basic building blocks of being a good human being," Fred said. "A tireless work ethic was something both my parents passed on to me. As a late bloomer I had struggles, you know, but I stuck with it and came out the other side academically. Also, I think a sense of humility is so important in life and to respect other people. I want to make sure they're grounded—that's something that I can pass on that I received from my father. Rowing has given me so much, because there's no hiding in this grueling team sport. There are no superstars. It's like the total teamwork demonstrated by *The Boys in the Boat*."

Fred shared a recent example of an aspiring rower applying to colleges who told him he had achieved a certain score on an indoor rowing machine used to test fitness. Fred found out the student had lied to him. "It's BS," Fred said, shaking his head. "I mean, he lied to me, but he's lying to himself. He's afraid. I believe in redemption, but he's going to have to turn it around. A friend of mine is a coach at Marietta College who's a philosophy major, and he talks about an analogy of a lamp. The shadow outside of the lamp shade is where you have to go as an athlete, into that pain cave. You have to be able to peer into that darkness and not be afraid to go there. Embrace the unknown. It's true in all sports. Some people take shortcuts. And some people refuse to take shortcuts—the successful ones."

Here I asked Fred for the number one thing. What was the most essential wisdom he felt would guide his grandkids, and ours, to become the greatest generation of all?

"In life," Fred said, "you're going to have so many ups and downs. Trust who you are and that you're going to figure it out. Just be resilient and keep marching forward. In grad school, I kept a piece of paper taped to my bulletin board with a saying from the German poet Goethe that read, 'Work and despair not.'"

Learning about Fred's life in rowing piqued my curiosity about the role of sports in shaping the lives of young people. I have to first acknowledge that athletics played only a small role in my own childhood. When I was in middle school, I won a silver ribbon in a shotput competition, but only because I was in detention and the assistant principal kicked me outside to compete in a track and field meet that was underway. I later joined the football team where, due to the fact that I was six foot six, they had me walk off the bus first at away games in the hopes that I would intimidate the opposing team. (That may have actually worked, because we were undefeated that season.) Sports just wasn't my thing. And yet through all my school years I had a feeling that I was missing out on something, that I was not part of a club that had its own exclusive benefits.

As parents, we made sure our son and daughter signed up for the teams of their choice (soccer/lacrosse/swimming), and every weekend we shuttled them to their games and joined the klatch of moms and dads rooting from the sidelines. It was tons of fun, and our kids got a lot out of it. I recall wondering now and then if one of my kids would double down on athletics and play college sports, or someday compete in the Olympics. Every parent envisions themselves in the bleachers bursting with pride as their grown child gets a perfect 10 after nailing a forward 4½ somersault off the high dive.

Today, as grandparents, those dreams have resurfaced as we cheer on our grandchildren when they kick the ball into the net. Whether they ever compete in the Olympics, however, is not my primary wish. I simply want them to learn what they can from sports in order to live their best lives. How can I help make that happen?

This is what led me to seek out the wisdom of a pro athlete grandpa. Thanks to an introduction by the leaders of Grandpas United, a nonprofit in White Plains, New York, that works with at-risk youth, I was soon face-to-face in Zoom-land with the great Reggie Williams. Reggie played fourteen seasons with the Cincinnati Bengals, won the NFL's Walter Payton Man of the Year Award in 1986, was named Co-Sportsman of the Year in 1987 by *Sports Illustrated,* and competed in two Super Bowl championships. After retiring from the NFL, he was hired by Disney to start their Wide World of Sports complex for aspiring young athletes. Today, Reggie is retired and lives in Orlando, Florida, where he can be near his five grandchildren. He has a smooth-shaven dome and neatly trimmed white beard.

When I talked with Reggie, I quickly learned that while his background was very different from Fred Schoch's, he has one big thing in common: the role his father played in shaping his life.

"My father, Elijah, was born and raised in Irondale, Alabama, just outside of Birmingham," Reggie said. "When he was sixteen, he had a tryout with Willie Mays for the Birmingham Black Barons. But his job wasn't playing baseball, it was working with field crews moving lumber and stuff like that. He knew how to drive a car, and one day he moved the truck closer to where the other men were working to make it easier for them to load the lumber into the truck. And the supervisor pulled my father out of the cab of the truck, because Negroes weren't allowed to drive, and my father hit him and thought he'd killed him. That night, he and all my uncles, they all had to leave Birmingham. So, he was on the road and the last stop before going to Canada was Flint, Michigan. My father could have been a pro athlete; our lives could have been completely different if he'd had a Willie Mays type of opportunity."

Elijah settled down in Flint, where he worked at an auto plant, got married, and started a family. Reggie was born in 1954, hearing impaired, and spent several years at the Michigan School for the Deaf. "If you can't hear sounds it's impossible to repeat those sounds," Reggie said, "so I developed a pretty good speech impediment."

I asked Reggie about his childhood trajectory into sports. "I think the first big accomplishment I ever had was the time I beat my father running," Reggie replied. "He was shocked. I was shocked. I realized I was fast and said to myself, *What am I going to do with this?*"

Reggie's home didn't have a basketball hoop in the driveway, but there was a big grass field nearby where he was taught how to play football by older kids in the neighborhood. By his senior year of high school, he was a starter on the varsity team, with dreams of getting an athletic scholarship. It was not to be. "Bo Schembechler was the head coach at the University of Michigan at the time—where I was offered an *academic* scholarship—and he met with my high school football coach," Reggie said. "Bo asked me to do him a favor and don't come out for the football team because I wasn't good enough. That really ruined my dreams and aspirations, but when I told my father about it, he said, 'Forget Bo!' I'd been accepted by Dartmouth College, but the Ivy league doesn't have athletic scholarships, so it would cost my father a lot more. He was already working hard, but he took a second job to pay for it. He basically said, 'Pursue your dreams.'"

Reggie enrolled at Dartmouth and made the football team in his freshman year. It didn't take him long to realize, however, that the racism that drove his father out of Birmingham had followed him to the hallowed halls of Dartmouth. "On the very first day of practice, there were these white kids from the South who didn't want to be in the same locker room or shower with me. And my head freshman coach, Jerry Berndt, found out about it and appointed me captain of the team; he instilled leadership in me; he took a chance on me, and I wanted to live up to his expectations. I became the most valuable player on the freshman team and the only Black All-American in the football program in Dartmouth's history."

When Reggie told me this story, I mentioned that—just by chance—we were having our conversation on Juneteenth. The Civil War and decades of Jim Crow injustice were part of our living history. "In my particular case," Reggie replied, "my father raised me to use all that as fuel to overcome adversity. That's the legacy of our family, the recognition that we are going to face this adversity and the question is, Are you prepared to overcome it?"

Going above and beyond on the playing field brought its own challenges. "I loved playing professional football for the Bengals," Reggie said, "but you get hurt a lot. I've had twenty-five knee operations and five knee replacements. One of the gifts of aging is to be relatively pain-free at this time in the company of happy, loving grandchildren. It's one of the best pain relievers." Reggie sees his grandchildren every week at his condo, going to the park or out to restaurants. And he's taken his grandkids to the local YMCA to teach them how to swim. I told Reggie that I learned how to swim when my Vermont cousins threw me in a lake without a life preserver. "You know," Reggie replied, "my kids would not even consider throwing a child into the water and saying, 'Go for it.' We came from the quote, unquote 'greatest generation,' the World War II generation. Seeing that scene in *Saving Private Ryan* of them storming the beaches at Normandy—there's just no way you can imagine how courageous it was."

I mentioned to Reggie that I had interviewed Tom Brokaw, author of *The Greatest Generation*, and Tom's belief that every generation had a shot at greatness. This branch of my discussion with Reggie led me back to the concept of adversity as fuel. I asked Reggie if there was one moment that stood out in his long NFL career where he had to ignite that fuel to win. I was expecting to hear about a desperate fourth-down play, a dash through the offensive line to sack the quarterback in the final seconds. But what I heard was far more riveting: "My last two years that I played for the Bengals, I was concurrently a Cincinnati city councilman. And while serving on the council I did something that was bigger than the fourteen years that I played for the Cincinnati Bengals. I had become friends with Arthur Ashe, and at that time he was boycotting all the tennis events in South Africa because of apartheid. And he's the one that told me about the opportunity to work consistently to end apartheid by having financial institutions divest from doing business in South Africa. So, I got our pension board for the city of Cincinnati to pass legislation that forced them to divest.

After that, I got a call from Archbishop Desmond Tutu, who said he wanted to come to Cincinnati and talk to me. When he visited, he told us that our legislation was the straw that broke the camel's back, that Nelson Mandela was getting out of Robben Island Prison and that South Africa was planning to have their very first democratic election, because I had turned off the last spigot of their financial relationship with the United States."

Reggie's time serving on the city council also included what he described as one of his biggest failures. "I was really passionate about trying to keep automatic weapons out of public schools," Reggie said. "This was before Sandy Hook and all the other massacres. It was the first time I ran into the NRA and their constituency. I'd played for the Bengals for eleven years. I'd been involved in community service my whole life. And the only time I've ever been called the N-word was after I tried to get that legislation to prohibit automatic weapons in public schools. It didn't pass."

Hearing this, I shared my sense of bewilderment and grief at the epidemic of school shootings. How was it possible that a country as great as ours could allow so many children to be slaughtered and do virtually nothing to stop it? Yet I hesitated to talk about guns in my book because the issue was so divisive in America today. Reggie leaned forward and said with deep conviction, "I think you've got to have some moral imperatives in your book. I mean, grandparents have to be cognizant of working towards resolving these issues."

I know Reggie is absolutely right. And I know, equally, that my spine could be tougher. I have to wonder if I lack the same kind of fuel that propelled Reggie through fourteen seasons in the NFL and dozens of injuries, not to mention standing up to the apartheid regime in South Africa. Nobody ever walked out of my locker room because of the color of my skin. I need to find my own fuel. For me, it has to be the love of my grandchildren and my belief—perhaps despite all evidence to the contrary—that they have a fighting chance to be the greatest generation. To that end, I asked Reggie for his number one wisdom for our grandchildren.

"It'd be simple," Reggie said. "Just be kind. Always gravitate to the kindness side of your heart, and better things will happen for you in the future. If everyone was kind, we could eliminate hate. That would be the most phenomenal world, a world that I strive for."

When I think about the things Fred and Reggie shared with me, there are more commonalities than differences. Fred said we need to instill in our grandchildren the understanding that they have the strength within them to "keep marching forward" no matter what, while Reggie—like his father before him—turned adversity into fuel and extolled the bright power of kindness. All these things help explain why great athletes train so hard, and why success on and off the field or waterway isn't just about winning per se. It's about doing the right thing for others. It's about having hope. This can be so very hard when we see yet another news story about a school massacre or some other preventable tragedy. It's so hard at times that we want to throw up our hands in despair. But if we "work and despair not," then all things are possible.

We grandparents have gray hair for a reason, and it's time we used it. We have been on this Earth a good long while and had our share of hardship and toil, and yet here we are, still kicking and able to raise our voices and take action to protect those we love and enable their best possible future. This is not some remarkable heroic thing on our part. There will be no accolades, no confetti on our faces as we walk victorious across the field. It's just what we'll do to support our team.

CHAPTER 9

Lifeboats in the Starry Night

When someone asks, "What's it like to be a grandpa?" the response is usually, "Fantastic! The best thing ever!" I've spoken with men who jumped for joy in the middle of a restaurant when they heard they were going to become grandpas. The whole world changes in a way that explodes outward. Many of us thought we could never love anyone, or any single thing, as much as our kids. Grandkids, however, take the cake.

Suddenly, the circle of those we care deeply about expands. Love expands. And the more grandkids we are lucky to have, the larger that circle of loving care becomes. But as with all things tied to this thing we call love there is complexity, and sometimes heartbreak. With each new addition to our family the possibility of pain and sorrow grows. The yin and yang of grandparenthood are inseparable. We know this is what we signed up for, which doesn't make it any easier.

People will say that sickness is part of life, but the truth is that sickness has a life of its own. Sickness is a bubbling cauldron of living bacteria, a cornucopia spilling over with every manner of infection. Sickness is a field of blossoming viruses, blood red and bobbing in the spring wind. These other forms of life, the uninvited guests that Poe described so horrifically in his short story "The Masque of the Red Death," are to us the ultimate party crashers, robbing us of the health we feel we are entitled to. And yet the bacteria and viruses are simply doing what all living things do, going about the business of living. They could easily protest that we are the ones crashing their party, when bodies give up and melt into the grass. We are, after all, literally the hosts of the party, and when our doors close they have no place to live. So, this battle goes on, and the toughest survive. Or the luckiest.

We all have our own stories to tell about familial hardship. I'll share one of mine.

The calls and texts from my daughter, Abigail, reached a crescendo over a period of days. First, my eldest grandson, Henry, had a cough. Then he had a bad cough. Then a *really bad* cough that was keeping him up all night. There was a worrisome rasping sound coming from his chest. A wheezing. A high fever that would not go away.

They took him to the emergency room, where Henry was diagnosed with RSV—a serious lower respiratory infection. They put him on oxygen. Put in an IV. Henry, flat on his back and listless, would recoil in speechless terror when the nurses came to take blood or check his vital signs. If he were older, he'd have full sentences to explain his fear like, "Why is this happening to me?" or "Who are these people who keep sticking me with needles?" But all he could do was scream.

My wife, Nancy, dropped everything and rushed to the hospital. I got a text from her that night that read, "Poor Henry is *so* sick." Nancy is a very grounded person by nature, not prone to worry, but I could hear the deep concern in her voice when we talked that night.

Most kids will get RSV before the age of two. Henry's case was particularly severe. When the nightmare of the needle-fingered nurses relented to sleep, his oxygen levels dropped dangerously low, even with an oxygen tube taped to his face. We were sent pictures of Henry in his hospital bed, or sleeping on Abigail's shoulder as she camped in a chair at 3:00 a.m. under the fluorescent lights that can make even healthy people look ill. The virus in Henry's chest was having a rager. A spring break. A ghoulish frat party. The more sickly the glow of the hospital lights, the brighter their revels.

It's at these moments when you ask yourself something you can't even think, and in conversations with your loved ones you can't say in words, so you speak around them with questions like, "How serious does the doctor say this is?" And the responses tend to trail off, the ellipses at the end of the sentence speaking volumes of dread. "Well, this happens to a lot of kids, and he'll probably be fine, but..."

This question is inevitable and natural. It's the one that's on the surface that we ask in conversation with our grown kids—the young parents toughing it out with our grandchildren. It's a question that goes deeper, though, much deeper, when we close our eyes and pray. I call myself a nonpracticing Unitarian, which some would say is redundant. Churches and dogmatic teachings never meant much to me. But when your grandkid is sick, there is a God. And if there is a God when your grandkid is sick, then there must always be a God. I reached out to God and asked for help in healing Henry. I did point out, in my very reasoned Unitarian way, that I rarely asked for help from the Divine. So maybe my solitary plea might be heard, as if God had some kind of spreadsheet that tallied the number of requests from mortals.

In my prayer, I pictured Henry in his hospital bed, sleeping. I was there above the whole scene creating a loving embrace that could let Henry know he was not alone in his fight to turn off the stereo at the all-night virus party. It was time for the partiers to go home. The cops were coming. They could continue their party someplace else, but this party was *over*.

I am convinced, through repeated experiences, that there is in fact a force of some kind that connects all of us, and it connects our families to an even greater extent, no matter where we are on Earth. Underscoring this connection is a river that holds all knowledge and awareness, a river that runs unseen beneath our conscious reality. All the answers are there. When we listen to it (very intently, shutting off the noise), we know what we need to know. This river doesn't use a lot of words, only the most important ones. That night, when I prayed for Henry—when I listened for Henry—I heard that he was going to be all right.

Three months later, I walked down to the beach on Lake Willoughby with Henry and Abigail. It was a cool early April day, the sky mostly cloudy. Half the lake was still covered in ice. The grass along the shore was still brown. Henry ran around happily in his bright orange coat, picking up sticks—"Sticks!"—and laughing as Abigail's dog, Rory, leapt into the freezing gray waves.

This story had a happy ending, but it's just one of many. How families band together in challenging times, including the recent pandemic, is central to the grandparenting life. I wondered how other grandpas navigate these troubled waters.

I set out to learn more.

My search led me to a coffee shop in Newton, Massachusetts, to talk with a grandpa named Eric Behr. I'd heard a little of Eric's story from my brother, Nick, who conducted him in the Mystic Chorale. And what Eric shared with me that day added a new dimension to my understanding of what it truly means to be a grandpa.

Eric Behr

Eric, seventy-six, is lean and fit, with a lined and thoughtful face, gray hair, and a melodious baritone voice that no doubt was a great addition to my brother's chorus. Eric is the father of three, grandfather of six, a successful folk musician, and newly retired accountant. I started our conversation at the beginning, diving into his family history, seeking to find the influences that helped shape him into who he is today.

Eric never knew his grandfathers (although he did recollect that a great-uncle survived the *Titanic*; that's a whole different story that may require its own book). Eric's father was outgoing and charismatic, a frustrated actor who finally found his stage as a diplomat, serving as the first liaison between the State Department and the Joint Chiefs of Staff. Quiet by nature, Eric's mother absolutely hated being a diplomat's wife. The two things Eric's parents had in common were that they were both listed in the *Social Register*, and both drank heavily.

Eric described his dad, Frederic Howell Behr, as a "world-class womanizer," made worse by the fact that he flaunted his infidelities. As Eric put it, "He rubbed my mother's nose in it." On more than one occasion, Frederic took his mistress on an overnight trip on the family yacht and brought Eric along.

"My parents were constantly screeching at each other," Eric said. When punishment was meted out by his parents, his dad used a belt, his mother a silver hairbrush.

"My childhood," he said, "was completely overcome with anxiety."

Eric's father died of lung cancer at the age of forty-one, when Eric was just fourteen. For Eric, this was a major rupture at a critical time of his life. Deeply flawed as his father was, the man still had a tremendous influence on him. "So, I walked away from God. I knew that God existed and God was supposed to be good, and when God took my father that was the end."

Bereft of spirituality, and inheriting his parents' love for booze, Eric struggled with addiction for decades. Attending college at Goddard with fellow students he described as "brilliant fuckups," Eric descended into a life of alcohol, drugs, and cigarettes. But Eric also did everything possible to turn his life around. He became committed to a rigorous twelve-step recovery program in 1986, and within a year he kicked alcohol and drugs for good.

Eric became a musician, cofounded and grew a successful accounting firm (what Eric calls his "side gig"), got married to his lovely wife, Nancy, and together raised their kids.

For Eric, the trauma of his childhood has informed his loving—and sober—approach to being a good parent and grandpa. He's been there for his grandkids' soccer games and all kinds of family gatherings. There is no screeching in his long marriage. And every new grandchild to appear on the scene has added a new layer to his happiness. His granddaughter, Molly, was born in 2017.

One sunny summer day in 2018 when the family was vacationing on Martha's Vineyard, Molly's mother, Cassy, noticed that her daughter was walking with her head tilted to one side. A doctor said the issue was likely muscular, but after further tests they heard the kind of news that every parent dreads. Molly had a rare form of brain tumor, an anaplastic ependymoma.

Surgeons were able to remove 98 percent of the tumor, but the remaining 2 percent was wrapped like a serpent around Molly's brainstem. No treatment known to mankind, in one of the best hospitals in the world, could fix this problem. The doctors could offer no hope for a cure, other than potentially keeping Molly alive long enough for new treatments to be developed.

Eric and his family were of course devastated. It's one thing to lose friends or family who are older to disease, but the prospect of losing a child is nearly unbearable.

Some people give up. It can be too easy to accept what doctors predict.

But for Eric and his wife, the crisis was a clarion call to dig deeper and find a way to break down the barriers to what's possible.

"Around the time Molly got sick I started listening to a Buddhist nun, Pema Chödrön," said Eric. "She got me thinking about energy—healing energy—and energy in general. Because when you break it all down to particles, that's all we are. Energy. And it seemed to me that was my path." Nancy enrolled in a school of energy medicine, and soon Eric joined her to learn all they could. At the same time, Nancy—an ordained pastor with a degree from Harvard Divinity School—began tapping into her network to let people know about Molly and pray for her. The effort started out small, but as word spread the circle grew and before long thousands of people were praying for Molly. Close family. Friends of friends. Complete strangers.

Molly underwent thirty-three rounds of proton radiation followed by metronomic chemotherapy. The goal of the chemo was simply to keep the tumor from growing. But when the follow-up scans were done, Molly's doctors where astonished to find the tumor had actually shrunk.

"They were stunned," Eric said. "They just didn't understand how that happened."

Eric and Nancy, however, did understand. "You've seen pictures of the sun with a gazillion rays, right?" Eric asked. "Each one of those is a way in and out of God." A man who had walked away from God at fourteen had found a new pathway in his seventies toward deep spirituality, a foundational energy with extraordinary power. Today, Eric starts each morning with a comprehensive program of yoga, meditation, reading, and prayer.

Five years after Molly's diagnosis she has defied all expectations. The tumor has not grown.

And yet challenges remain. In July of 2022, Molly came down with a pneumonia that very nearly took her life. During her monthlong hospital stay, bloodwork showed that she had developed chemotherapy-induced acute myeloid leukemia. Once again, the family persevered. Molly received a bone marrow transplant from her mother. After more months in the hospital, Molly finally came home in the winter, living in a virtual bubble to avoid infection.

In November of 2023, happy and smiling and for all the world seeming normal and healthy, Molly went back to school.

Before Eric and I parted ways, I asked him the question I ask of all grandpas. "If you picture yourself years in the future and you're talking to Molly and your other grandkids, what would you say? The number one thing?"

Eric thought for a moment, then said, "Trust yourself. Trust your instincts. Your life is your responsibility. It doesn't help you or anybody to blame the way you're feeling on somebody else."

"The childhood they are going to have," Eric explained, "is much briefer than the one you and I had. And that's predominantly driven by the internet. I'm scared to death of the crap that's available on computer screens." For Eric—and I suspect for many grandparents—it's startling to realize that we worry more about toxic media than cancer. What does this say about the direction of our modern hyper-technology-driven world?

Today, Eric spends lots of time with his grandkids, practicing mindfulness to be fully present. All of his storied ancestry and life experience is built into the fabric of his being. It's a quilt comprised of many individual ideas and values. It's loving, loyal, and steady. It's sober and powerful and spiritual. There's joy, laughter, pain. A gospel chorus that gives you chills. A map for doing the right thing. A soul that will always find ways for family to survive, and never give up trying. No matter what awaits, there's always a lifeboat available somewhere in the starry night. You just have to pray.

CHAPTER 10

Letters from Saba

In the early twelfth century, Judah ben Saul ibn Tibbon, a translator and physician living in Southern France, picked up his pen to write a letter. He was likely an old man at the time, wise and perhaps frail, fully aware of the limited amount of sand remaining in his life's hourglass. His words were not meant to be read by friends or business associates. It was a letter to be read in the future by his children and grandchildren:

> Avoid bad society, make thy books thy companions, let thy book-cases and shelves be thy gardens and pleasure-grounds. Pluck the fruit that grows therein, gather the roses, the spices, and the myrrh. If thy soul be satiate and weary, change from garden to garden, from furrow to furrow, from sight to sight. Then will thy desire renew itself, and thy soul be satisfied with delight.[3]

Judah's letter was a form of ethical will, an ancient Jewish tradition that dates back to biblical times. The practice of passing on accrued wisdom to nurture future generations, these written time capsules, became more broadly used through the Middle Ages and in time was adopted by people of all faiths, continuing into our modern era.

Here, I must pause to ask my father's favorite question: Why?

I've seen the answer written on the faces of the many grandpas I've recently interviewed. Very few of the men I've spoken with (all of them boomers like me) ever had a chance to know one of their grandpas. The actuarial tables show why this is the case. An American man born in 1900 had an average life expectancy of about forty-seven years.[4] By the time their children had children most of them were no longer on the scene. An ethical will, often referred to as a Forever Letter, is an insurance policy against the loss of the precious ideas and values we pray our grandchildren will learn from us. We yearn for the chance to guide our grandchildren and leave a lasting legacy.

The history of the Forever Letter was brought home to me by a grandpa who has become a friend, Bob Halperin. Bob reached out to me after reading my blog, and we met up at the local Starbucks Grandpa Networking Center, and for subsequent fast hikes on ice-covered nature trails. Bob, I quickly learned, is a fascinating guy. He earned his undergraduate degree in economics from Brandeis, an MBA from Harvard Business School, and went on to lead a range of learning-focused organizations, notably serving as director of the MIT Sloan Executive Education program. Today, Bob runs his own consulting practice that provides support groups for senior executives.

Bob and I have different educational backgrounds (his is better) but have the same haircut (bald) and share an interest in family stories. Bob, sixty-eight, speaks animatedly to convey ideas that spark out of his prodigious mind like intellectual popcorn. He's also a writer, and a good one. While he didn't know his grandfathers, one of them—Morris Jacobsohn—nevertheless left a big impression on him. "In 1950," Bob said, "he wrote a letter to my oldest cousin, David, and I got to read it when I was twelve."

Bob shared the letter with me. It begins:

> I am addressing this letter to you. Being the oldest, the first of our grandchildren, you will reach maturity and fuller understanding before all your cousins. My request: please impart the contents of this letter to them, as they reach the age of full understanding.

Morris went on to describe his early childhood growing up impoverished in Palestine before it was Israel, his learning Hebrew at the age of three and a half, and studying the Talmud at age six. Morris poured his soul into sharing a structure for how his grandchildren should live:

> In this outline, I hope to impart to you my personal code for living. I consider this code, not merely my ethical foundation, but the very cause of my humble attainments in life.

His lifelong love of scripture featured prominently in the formation of his personal code:

> Studying the Bible in the original Hebrew, I was trained to reach a broader understanding of "How and Why" of human actions and progress.

Morris finishes with words that spoke to Bob as if he were in the same room with him, because, in a way, he was:

> One wishes to be remembered well. And in the hope that you will all so remember me, I conclude this letter with my final wishes; may you all share good opportunities and good fortune all through your lives.

Inspired by his grandfather's example, Bob started writing letters to his two daughters when they were young, each letter designed to share his love and wisdom to mark a milestone in their lives such as graduating from high school or having their first child. When Bob's first grandchild was born, he set up a special Gmail address from Grandpa Bob. As of today, he's written about forty emails to his three grandchildren, collectively called "Letters from Saba" (Hebrew for "grandfather"). "They're written in an adult way for them to read when they're older," Bob said, "and I've told my daughters, 'Here's the email address, here's the password. I could die at any time, but they're there.'"

Bob shared some of the letters with me, starting with this introduction:

> This is the first of what I hope will be many emails I will send to you over the coming months and years! It may be many years before you can fully understand all of my messages. I will leave it to your parents to decide how and when to share with you.

And an email with a playful lesson on gratitude:

> One small way that I try to remember to be grateful for even the smallest things I have is by saying what orthodox Jews call *Asher Yatzar* (or informally the "Peeing Prayer").

Plus other emails addressing some of life's most profound challenges:

> The reality of life is that you will be blessed to have people in your life that you love and respect, and can't imagine living without. And then through accident or illness, they will be taken away from you. I cannot shield you from these hard realities, but I can offer some perspective, having lived through my own losses.

I found Bob's letters to be charming and smart. How cool is it that a tradition that dates back to biblical times is now in email form? While Saba's letters were written to his grandchildren, they also spoke to me. The more I thought about Letters from Saba, the more I thought of my own family and our legacy. I remembered a letter that my dad had written to my four older brothers a few years before I was born. The first time I read it I was in my early twenties, when my dad was still with us, and I recall thinking it was lovely, but not life-altering. After talking with Bob, I tracked down the letter and when I read it again—as a sixty-four-year-old grandpa—it resonated profoundly. My dad passed away in 2011, and reading this brought him back to me, vividly. But I also had to live longer to more fully appreciate the depth and beauty of his wisdom. Here is the letter.

> July 2, 1956
>
> To my Children:
>
> When you get old enough to understand this letter fully, you will be as old as I am, but I hope you will keep it, Calvin, so that you and the others may read it later on. Dear Calvin, Charles, Bill Jr. and John: There are times when I wished I knew what my father thought. It wasn't that I wanted to lean on him for advice but it's just that I always felt that he was a man that I would have liked to have known better. I expect to be around a long time after you have grown up, but I want to talk to you now.
>
> I've just finished flying across the country—to San Francisco and then to Los Angeles and Denver where I bought your mother an Aspenwood pin, and some gold nuggets for you fellas—and then back to Boston. I know that you will all take this air trip some day and when you do, I know you will feel as I did that it is a tremendous and fascinating experience—where the grandeur of these United States perceived in a brief span of hours brings the meaning of unity home—unity of the land and the people and the weather and the soil. Nature shouts out to you, "This is what I am." And our people say, "Fine, this is what you are. Here is what I can do to change you—to make you do something for me and my fellow Americans. Nature, I

have the most powerful tool in the world—it's the cooperation I get from my fellow citizens. They are my partners and if your soil grows plants and your mountains give minerals and if your waters carry boats and generate power and quench people's thirst, it is because they are partners."

I looked down, near sunset, on the tiny town of Delta surrounded by the vast desert of Utah. Off on the edge of town on a hill was a Mormon church. The people of the town had planted the hill with green grass and connected up lights on the lawn to illuminate the outside of the church. And with the sands of the desert mixing with the grass at the bottom of the hill, one of the greatest symbols of man's unity shone brightly and gloriously in the dusk.

One of the things that will impress you when you fly across the country is the progress that people have made and the potential for the progress that has yet to come. You are all going to take part in that progress and your contributions to that progress will influence the lives of each of your other fellow Americans. Here is the challenge that comes with being born a United States citizen. You have more tools at your disposal here than anywhere in the world—more knowledge, more education, more cooperating and effective people to work with, and a more responsive and better loved governmental system than the citizens of any other country in the world.

The challenge to each of you is all the greater because you have these things with which to work. What are some of the things that challenge you Calvin and you Charles and you Bill and you John. When you read this letter later on, you will be able to state them as well as I.

1. The successful completion of a world community where the same cooperative spirit that exists across the United States exists throughout the world.
2. The elimination of disease.
3. The pushing back of boundaries of scientific knowledge, both in the physical and the social fields, and the application

of that knowledge for the good of everybody who breathes oxygen and those yet to breathe it (your children).

You will come to know that the greatest contribution that each of you shall make to this progress shall come by using your minds—by thinking. The greatest contributions to human welfare are not made by those who serve the people, but by those who determine how to serve. One of the most important contributors to the progress of the United States had this to say, "The man who doesn't make up his mind to cultivate the habit of thinking misses the greatest pleasure in life. He not only misses the greatest pleasure, but he cannot make the most of himself. All progress, all success, springs from thinking." That was Thomas Edison.

When you grow older, read. Read Edison's biography, his own notes, Ernest Dimnet's "The Art of Thinking," Osborn's "Applied Imagination," Leonardo da Vinci's "Notebooks," Newton's "Principia," Abraham Lincoln's letters, Bertrand Russell's "A History of Western Philosophy." Read what you love to read. Great men will speak to you. You can get their thoughts for the price of a book.

Calvin and Charles and Bill and John, feel deeply the value and the purpose of the thing you are striving to create. Question, question, question! What is it good for? Who will benefit? How? When? Where? Why?

Each of you will come to feel that you have a great task before you. Be a fighter. Choose your weapons carefully and fight. Find more pleasure in intelligent dissent than in passive agreement, for, if you value intelligence as you should, the former implies a deeper agreement than the latter. And remember, that the most powerful weapon in the world is clear thought.

With all my love to you boys,

Dad

What immediately struck me after reading this was my dad's heartfelt portrayal of America. I could barely recognize his positive 1956 vision of our country versus the toxic, divisive mess we live in today. How and why has America come to this juncture, and what can we do about it? How can our grandkids have any hope of becoming the next great generation if our country lacks a hopeful unifying vision for the future?

It wasn't until Bob shared with me his number one wisdom that an answer, a sliver of light, began to gleam in my darkness.

Bob smiled and said, "Rabbi Hillel was asked to summarize the Torah standing on one foot, and what he says is some version of the Golden Rule: Do unto others as you would have them do onto you; the rest is commentary. Now, go study! So, my first answer to your question is, try to be a good listener. Because if you can be a good listener, the rest is commentary, right? If you can be a good listener, everything else is possible."

When I read my dad's letter—and the letters from Bob's saba—with this in mind, it brought home to me that conveying wisdom in our ethical wills is only the beginning. What matters is actually listening to the amazing things that are written, and then taking action. I had read my dad's guidance to think and read, I had seen the list of books he told us to read, but I'd never read them. Last week I went to the library and took out Bertrand Russell's *History of Western Philosophy* and Leonardo da Vinci's *Notebooks,* and I'm devouring them like a man who's been starving in the wilderness. I'm listening to Bob's saba's advice, too, and will finally read the Bible (the whole thing versus the bits I read in Sunday school). And I'm saying the Peeing Prayer on a regular basis!

I've started conversations with my children about what it means to be American, and we are planning a family trip with all the grandkids to visit the Statue of Liberty. I want them to know that America can still be a beacon of hope to the world—if we get our act together. I'll tell them that I have traveled to many countries, and they are great countries, but to this day I would still choose to live in the US, despite its many flaws, because we are the only country that has a dream—the American dream. Anything is possible here. Anything. But to Bob's point, the full range of what's possible depends on our ability to listen to each other. We may not agree with the political views of others, but that doesn't make them bad people. We can find pleasure—and ultimately common ground—through thoughtful conversations and intelligent dissent, versus bloodthirsty cage matches on Facebook and cable news. In his letter to his grandsons Saba Morris wrote it better than I can: "Broad-mindedness, as against being fanatic or addicted to habits and ideas, leads on to the correct fashioning of one's own life. Tolerance and patience, as added virtues, help to prevent much of bitterness and suffering, from disappointments and frictions with society and surroundings."

The writing of letters meant to be read by future generations has one additional and critically important value. Simply writing down our thoughts helps to crystalize them *today*. For me, this entire book is a letter to my grandchildren, all the richer thanks to the wonderful ideas other sabas have shared with me. If indeed the most powerful weapon in the world is clear thought, I hope the collective wisdom here will prove in time to be an arsenal that unleashes extraordinary potential. Question, question, question! If the answers don't come to us right away, we'll keep trying and never give up. We'll fight like hell, because this dream is worth it.

CHAPTER 11

The Forever Story

Once upon a time in a land far away and long ago, my dad used to make up stories for us at bedtime. All his stories involved the same seven characters: Casper, Jasper, and five boys named Calvin, Charlie, Nick, John, and Ted—me and my four older brothers. I recall loving the stories, but that's all I remember because they were never written down.

When my two kids were little, I took a page from my dad's dreamtime creative playbook and made up my own stories to tell them at bedtime. My kids remember loving the stories, but that's all they remember because I never wrote them down.

These days, coming up with stories that feature my grandkids is as wonderful for me as it is for them, and maybe I've finally learned my lesson because I've started writing them down. My grandkids jump into bed and implore me, "Grandpa, tell us a story!" Then—like the grandpa in *The Princess Bride*—I spin a tale of magical adventures. I'll often pause in the middle of a story to offer up different branching pathways and give the grandkids a choice of which way to go, or ask them to create and vote on the best solution for beating the dragon, crossing the fiery swamp, or outwitting the ogre.

Of course, it's inevitable that they get so excited that going to sleep is impossible. I completely fail at the "get the kids calmed down" concept, and I've taken some heat for it. I beg forgiveness. Many years from now, my grandkids will never remember that they lost a few hours of sleep, but they will remember the stories I told them and the special time we had together. These are Forever Stories, cut from the same cloth as Forever Letters but with a creative twist.

Here's a recent tale:

Lucinda had been playing with her teddy bears—Henry, Charlie, Roen, and Mae—for much of the afternoon on a green spring day in the little town of Oakdale, Connecticut, when she yawned very wide and said, "Oh goodness."

Lucinda's mom, Fern, called up from downstairs just at that moment, "Lucinda! Time for your nap!"

Lucinda gave her bears a big hug and a kiss and set them down side by side in the playroom. "Sleep tight, my fair princes," she said. Lucinda's mom tucked her into bed, and soon the little girl fell into a deep sleep.

But in the playroom, things were just starting to wake up. In the dimness, a small red light blinked on and a man's voice crackled over a radio. "Calling all Teddy Bear Rescue Squads. Calling all Teddy Bear Rescue Squads. Can you read me?"

The bears jumped to their feet and ran to the radio. Charlie pressed the red button and whispered, "Squad one reporting! I repeat, squad one reporting! Over."

"Roger that, squad one!" said the voice. "We need you down at the playground immediately! A tiger has gotten loose from the zoo, and if he's not put back in his cage, who knows what could happen!"

"No problem!" said Henry. "We're on it, Chief!"

"Let's go!" piped up Roen, a girl bear.

"Let's go!" chimed in Mae, Roen's little sister, who was learning how to talk and often repeated whatever her sister said.

The bears had a quick meeting, trying to keep their teddy bear voices down. In case you've never heard a teddy bear talk, it's a very high pitch, almost like hearing a baby ask for crackers or something. Use your imagination.

The question now was, Should they take the Rescue Squad race car, the minijet, or the hot air balloon?

"This is my thinking," said Charlie. "If we take the minijet we might get there faster, but there's no place to land at the playground. The race car would be pretty fast, but if we take the hot air balloon we can bring the animal cage to put the tiger in. The cage won't fit in the car."

"Excellent idea!" said Henry, a little too loudly apparently, for they suddenly heard footsteps in the hall getting closer to their door. The bears jumped back to sit exactly where Lucinda had left them and sat very still, trying to make their glass eyes look blank so that if Fern peeked in she wouldn't suspect that they were real live bears with a secret mission in the Teddy Bear Rescue Squad.* They heard the footsteps stop just outside the door, as if Fern had paused to listen, but then they moved on.

"Quick!" Henry whispered.

"Yea," Charlie whispered back, "before anyone spots us!"

"'I'll bring some blueberries!" said Roen, who always enjoyed snacks even during emergencies.

* Just out of curiosity I recently Googled "Teddy Bear Rescue Squad" and discovered that a woman in England is making creative clothes for a Teddy Bear Rescue Squad. Small world.

They grabbed the hot air balloon from the closet and hung it out the window, then used the air machine to pump air into the balloon, which quickly grew in size. Then they attached the red-and-blue-striped basket to the bottom of the balloon with ropes, and below that they hung the animal cage. Within minutes they were floating above the house and over the trees as the wind blew them toward the school playground.

Charlie used the spyglass to navigate. "Left, twenty degrees!" he ordered. "Good, now down a bit—*watch out for that tree!*" They barely missed hitting the top of a big oak tree with its branches that seemed to reach out like hands.

"Look!" Henry squeaked as he peered through the spyglass, "The tiger!"

"Let me see!" Charlie said, taking hold of the spyglass. "Wow!"

Roen had her turn, too. "That's a big tiger!" she said when she saw the yellow-and-black-striped beast pacing next to the swing set, its tail swishing side to side.

"That's a big tiger!" Mae said.

Mrs. Moore, one of the teachers at the school, was perched on top of the swing set clutching the metal bar for dear life, staring down at the tiger pacing hungrily below.

The squad arrived over the playground and hovered there as they worked out a plan. How would they get the tiger into the cage to save Mrs. Moore?

"I could blast it with my stun rocket," Henry suggested.

"I could make it fall asleep by shooting it with an arrow tipped with sleeping powder!" said Charlie.

"Let's cast a magic spell!" Roen said.

Mae stomped her cowboy boots and shouted, "I'll kick it in the face!" Everyone looked at Mae, wondering when she'd learned to say something like that and how the tiger would respond if kicked in the face by Mae's boot with its silver sparkles and a picture of Elsa from *Frozen*.

All these ideas *could* work, they decided, but were a bit risky.

Roen got out her blueberries to have a snack, offering a bowl of them to the rest. They munched the sweet blueberries for a minute, thinking hard to make the right decision. Then Roen had an epiphany, which is like an idea that pops into your head. "I'll put my blueberries into the cage so the hungry tiger will go in and eat them. Then we'll slam the door shut!"

Mae piped in, "Then we'll slam the door shut!"

"Yes!" Henry said, pumping the air with his furry brown fist. "That's how Grandpa Ted catches groundhogs. If it works for groundhogs, it'll work for a tiger!"

"But do tigers eat blueberries?" asked Charlie.

"There's only one way to find out!" Henry said.

"Find out!" Mae said.

Roen was lowered down on a rope toward the cage, which was hanging below the hot air balloon. Being as careful as possible, she attached a bag of blueberries to one side of the cage with tape. Henry and Charlie hauled her back up and she plopped down into the air balloon's basket. "I've never done *that* before," Roen said breathlessly.

"Well done, Roen!" Charlie and Henry said.

"Well done, Roen!" Mae said.

They positioned the hot air balloon directly over the tiger and—bit by bit—lowered the cage down to the playground. When Mrs. Moore saw them, her eyes filled with wonder because teddy bears flying around in balloons is not something you see every day.

The tiger looked up and growled, "Who is this who dares disturb my snack time?" But when the tiger saw the cage and walked toward it, he grew curious. He walked into the cage slowly, farther and farther, sniffing the bag of blueberries.

The tiger growled, "Is it meat?"

"No," said Roen.

"Is it cheese pizza?"

"No," said Charlie.

The tiger licked the outside of the bag, curiously. "Is it candy?"

"Much better than candy!" said Henry.

"Much better than candy!" Mae said.

This is when Roen took out her ukulele and sang her blueberry song, "Blueberry, blueberry, bluuuuuuuue... berry!"

The tiger could not resist. With one giant chomp he bit the whole bag of blueberries right off the back of the cage and chewed, a look of heavenly satisfaction spreading across his big cat face.

Quick as a wink Charlie pulled a rope that snapped that cage shut.

Oh, the tiger did not like being trapped one bit. He roared, blueberries clinging to his long fangs as he bit the bars of the cage in vain. Mrs. Moore, however, was delighted. She jumped down off the swing set and looked up in gratitude as the balloon—now towing the furious tiger inside the cage—rose up into the sky.

"Who, er, *what* are you?!" she called up to them.

"We're the Teddy Bear Rescue Squad!" they shouted.

Henry, Charlie, Roen, and Mae flew over to the zoo and lowered the cage down inside, then fast as birds they fluttered their way back home, let the air out of the balloon, and crawled back through a window. It was good they did, because just after they'd sat down in the pile of other toys, Fern (who thought she'd heard something) popped her head into the room. But all she saw was four teddy bears sitting absolutely still.

The zoo was grateful to have their tiger back. They set it loose in their African savanna area so it could roam around freely. What the zookeepers could never figure out, though, was why the tiger never wanted to eat the bowls of red meat they put in his cage. All the tiger would eat was fresh fruit, brought in by the truckload.

Over time, the zoo bought four more tigers to add to its collection. On any given day, though, you can easily tell which of them is the tiger that terrorized Mrs. Moore in the playground. It's the one sitting, its belly stuffed, in a pile of banana peels and bits of blueberries, apples, oranges, grapes, and mangos. On Thursdays he gets a special treat of pineapples, which he eats in one gulp. He never ate meat again. Kids visiting the zoo named him Fruity the Tiger.

It turns out my practice of making up stories that star my grandkids is not at all unique. Lots of grandpas do this, and one in particular—Andre Renna, from Lancaster, Pennsylvania—took the idea to a whole new level. Andre reached out to me through my blog, and we had a great conversation in Zoom-land where I learned about his family roots and his storybook grandpa creations. Andre, seventy, is a retired engineer and health-care manager who grew up in a classic Italian American family in Bensonhurst, Brooklyn. "I had the greatest childhood in the world," Andre told me. "My cousins lived in the house with me. We'd sit on the porch and watch the Mets on TV and have some espresso and sweet pastry. I'd walk to my grandmother's house four blocks away." Andre's dad was his hero, a solid presence in his life who worked multiple jobs to make sure there was always food on the table, with Italian feasts served up by his mom. Andre had a close relationship with both his grandfather, a bricklayer, and his grandmother. "I inherited some of my grandfather's tools—trowels, a hammer," Andre said. "Those things are precious to me." The number one wisdom Andre wants to share with the next generation is rooted in what his family taught him all those years ago in Brooklyn—*never break a promise*. "Your word," he said, "is the most important thing you have."

Andre and his wife raised their two kids in Lancaster, and today they have two grandkids. His granddaughter, Aria, arrived on the scene first, launching a wonderful new chapter in Andre's life. "She is without a doubt the light of my life," Andre told me. "Everyone else is a close second."

When Aria was eighteen months old, she won a stuffed yellow duck at a seaside boardwalk arcade. Aria's Ducky became a much-loved companion that she carried everywhere—even into her imagination. One day when Aria was five, Andre was pushing her on the swing. "And she says, 'I want to have a surprise birthday party for Ducky.' And then she disappears because I'm pushing her and she's still talking, right? We were on the swing for forty-five minutes, and she told me this whole story..."

"Everyone will be at the party," Aria said. "Penguin, Turtle, Unicorn..."

WHOOSH!

"Flamingo, Snakey, and T-Rex and..."

WHOOSH!

"But Jasmine the cat is going to ruin the party..."

WHOOSH!

"In the end Ducky will be OK because he knows we really love him."

When they went inside, Andre excitedly told his wife the whole story. His wife told him, "Why don't you write it as a book?"

Andre replied, "What the heck do I know about writing a children's book?"

"Just do it!"

When Andre related this, I was reminded that the smartest thing we can do as grandpas is listen to our wives. Andre immediately went to work, embarking on a remarkable collaboration with Aria to create a new children's book, *The Surprise Birthday Party: The Adventures of Aria and Ducky,* featuring a little girl named Aria and her menagerie of animals. He started by simply writing down the story Aria had shared with him; she, along with Andre's wife and sister, offered up suggestions and corrections to polish the draft. Andre then hired a professional illustrator, David Leonard, to bring the story to life.

The Surprise Birthday Party: The Adventures of Aria and Ducky, *a collaboration between Andre Renna and his granddaughter, Aria.*

For Andre and Aria, the smallest details mattered. Aria would review the working drafts and say things like, "That doesn't look like Ducky" or "Jasmine the cat is the wrong color." Andre was diligent about making sure that the Aria character looked just like the real Aria, from facial features to blond hair. "I said to the illustrator it has to look like her because I want to be able to say, 'That's my granddaughter.' And in the future I want her to be able to show this to her kids and grandkids. I drove him nuts."

It was worth it. Andre gave me a copy of the book, and it is lovely. When the book launched, Andre and Aria did their own promotional push, appearing on local TV stations and doing interviews for newspapers. While Andre has sold numerous

Andre with Aria and her Ducky.

books, he's found a bigger audience by donating them to pediatric hospitals.

The genesis of the book, with characters based on toys and featuring real children, will have a familiar ring to students of classic children's literature. Winnie-the-Pooh came about when English author A. A. Milne was inspired by a stuffed bear toy that he had bought for his son, Christopher Robin. But whether *The Adventures of Aria and Ducky* ever becomes well known doesn't ultimately matter, and the same is true for the Teddy Bear Rescue Squad. What does matter is that these stories have a chance to become classics in the lives of our families.

I think about the magic of storytelling a lot when I ponder what our grandkids will need in order to become the greatest generation. Many children live in a world of imagination. The couch cushions are their castle walls, a chopstick is Harry Potter's magic wand. But somewhere along the line—perhaps when they are lined up in rigid rows at school—their flights of fancy become grounded, their creativity stymied by the need to pass the next test. Yet the truth is that being creative throughout their entire lives may be the ultimate test, the best thing they can bring to their own families, and indeed to employers. The World Economic Forum's *Future of Jobs Report* found that creative-thinking skills is a top priority when considering talent.[5] Artificial intelligence will eat a billion jobs, but the careers of genuinely creative people will be secure for all time.

If we follow the example of Andre and Aria, and A. A. Milne, the next generation will always have their secret forest to walk in, their Hundred Acre Wood, a place where wise owls talk, where the mysterious Heffalump eludes even the best trackers, and our favorite bear devours pots of delicious honey. Ducky, Casper, Jasper, Christopher Robin, Calvin, Charlie, Nick, John, and Ted will also live in the forest, plus my grandkids and yours, forever and ever.

And that, oh my best beloved, is the end of the story.

CHAPTER 12

The Profitable Lemonade Stand

One Christmas, a year when three of my brothers were in college, my parents were feeling strapped due to the simultaneous tuition payments. These days, most people would take out college loans. Not then. We came downstairs Christmas morning to see the usual festively wrapped boxes under the tree. When we opened them, we found that each was empty except for a note card with an IOU; mine read "IOU one Monopoly Board Game," signed, "Love, Mom & Dad." It turned out to be my favorite Christmas ever because I'd been missing my brothers terribly, and it was great to have them home for the day.

A few years after the IOU Christmas, my mom discovered that a large bag of brown rice she'd purchased many months ago was crawling with worms. I begged her to throw it out, but she refused. "It's perfectly good rice!" she said, handing me and my brothers tweezers to pick out the wriggling worms—a maddening task because the worms were the exact same color and size as a grain of brown rice.

Christmas present boxes containing only IOUs (inset).

My parents' extreme frugality manifested itself throughout my childhood, including my dad's habit of draping used paper towels to dry in the kitchen so he could use them again later, my mom making her own clothes at her Singer sewing machine, and my having to wear only hand-me-down shoes. Growing up, my feet were often scrunched in shoes one or two sizes too small for me, resulting in permanent hammertoe. All this despite the fact that my dad was a successful executive with Polaroid. We weren't poor. We just acted that way. Having scraped by in the Great Depression, my parents saw waste as a cardinal sin and saving money as godly in some agnostic Unitarian way. Within the mythology of Brokaw's greatest generation, being cheap was a powerful weapon in the battle for a better life.

Having lived like a sharecropper as a child, I swore my kids would indeed have a better life, even if I went broke making it happen. When our daughter was in middle school, she begged us to go on a trip led by an organization called People to People, founded by President Dwight Eisenhower to foster better relations among countries. We ponied up over $3,000—a lot for us back then. And the country Abigail visited to improve America's global relations? Australia.

My wife and I have been knuckleheads in many ways with our money (or lack thereof), but we did save on the road to retirement thanks to a recurring character in this book: my Gramp. I never inherited money from him. I did, however, learn lessons that I've taken to the bank.

Gramp was an independent sales rep who traveled around New England selling retail displays from the trunk of his car. These were the early days of three-dimensional plastic signage that could be affixed to glass storefronts. (For some reason the penguin smoking a cigarette display stuck in my mind.) Gramp made decent money. Once when talking with me about investing, he grinned and said with a wink, "Oil stocks." All through the 1950s and beyond he invested in the booming postwar energy sector. When he retired, he could afford to keep the family farm in Vermont and buy a nice condo in Tucson, Arizona.

Earlier in the book I wrote about the first grandparents thirty thousand years ago, the ones who began the tradition of teaching their kids and grandkids the everyday tips needed to survive and thrive. The wisdom imparted by these grandparents had a cascading impact as more and more techniques for living longer and more successful lives became broadly shared.

What are the seed-planting tips of our time that will help our grandkids become the greatest generation? One area they need help with, desperately, is finance. The United States is considered a wealthy nation. Yet roughly half of Americans aged sixty-five and older get at least 50 percent of their family income from Social Security, and a quarter of them get 90 percent.[6] The Social Security Administration projects that the funds will run out by 2041.[7] In that year my youngest granddaughter will be nineteen.

My wife and I never seemed to have much left over after paying for things like the kids' braces—not to mention my daughter's visit to the Great Barrier Reef to repair relations with the Australians—but we put away at least *some* money each year in our retirement plans. Following Gramp's independent work example, I started my first company—a housecleaning business—when I was in high school. Getting paid to clean toilets felt like magic. I was literally turning shit into gold, and I could set my own hours. After beginning my career as a copywriter with an ad agency in New York City, I founded my own marketing agency and never looked back.

And now—shazam—all these grandkids are running around. Unfortunately, personal finance is generally not taught in schools. Which means it's up to the parents and grandparents to get the job done. How, I wondered, could I as a grandpa help them learn from me as I learned from Gramp, but take it up a notch? Maybe, like a second language, finance—and especially entrepreneurship—is best learned in childhood.

While I was ruminating on this idea, I happened to be visiting my daughter and her boys one fall day when they decided to set up a lemonade stand. Everyone threw in ideas for getting started. Abigail and her husband, Ryan, said they could pick up some lemonade mix and cups at Costco. The boys would make a sign. A card table was carried up from the basement.

I said to the boys, "Make sure you write down the cost of the lemonade and cups so you can keep track of your profits."

"What?" they said in unison through mouths full of breakfast.

"It's not about how much lemonade you sell," I explained, "it's about how much money you actually make per cup of lemonade after you take your cost of goods into consideration. The money you have after you subtract your expenses for lemonade and cups will equal your profit."

The boys stared at me, chewing, digesting this concept thoughtfully.

"Ordinarily," I went on, "you'd have to pay someone to sell the lemonade for you. That would be your cost of labor, and you'd have to subtract that from your profit, too, but since you'll be selling it yourselves you won't have to pay anyone else."

After some initial head-scratching they were all over the idea of making a profit. When Ryan returned from Costco with the supplies, the boys examined the receipt and did the math, then we discussed how much they should charge per cup of lemonade in order to be profitable.

Like Tom Sawyer painting the fence, my grandsons were soon joined by a gaggle of boys and girls in the neighborhood. Before long they were all hopping up and down with their sign to get cars to pull over—which they did, in droves. At one point, the kids flagged down a fire truck from the local fire station. Grinning and evidently thirsty firemen hung out with the kids, and my grandsons got to try on their helmets.

The cost per cup was set at fifty cents, but nearly everyone paid a full dollar. As the afternoon wore on, the bills in their bucket grew like leafy green plants in a fast-motion time-lapse film. Stepping back from it all, seeing them boisterous and laughing in the sun, I saw these boys and girls growing in fast motion, too, sprouting up before my eyes. They had one foot in childhood, the other in the business school of life. They rocked it!

But the ultimate finance lesson came from their dad. Ryan encouraged them to set aside a percentage of their lemonade-stand profits to donate to the local fire department. What a fantastic lesson: pull money out of thin air, make people happy with a refreshing beverage, *earn* a video game versus begging for it, and allocate a percentage of profits to help others. Capitalism is by no means perfect, but at its best it is a great engine of prosperity *and* charity. The Captains of Industry of the Gilded Age built their vast summer "cottages" in Newport, Rhode Island. Yet they also established philanthropic organizations that to this day benefit millions of people every year. Paul Newman donated 100 percent of his Newman's Own profits to charities. (He famously said, "Give it all away!") Bill Gates is leading a charge to support children's health globally.

To create positive change in their lifetimes, our grandkids need not become fabulously wealthy. They can start by simply making a decent living, regardless of the color of their skin or what town they grow up in, and along the way do the small things that matter—like donations to local charities. The littlest gestures repeated by millions of young people will add up to their better world. We can help put this power in their hands, one cup of profitable lemonade at a time.

Entrepreneurship is part of the overall financial literacy equation, but it's not enough. I'm not an expert in this. In fact, what I *don't know* about finance could fill a book. So, I sat down to talk with a grandpa who knows a great deal about finance, Jack Moore, my son-in-law's father, who was with our grandsons that day helping with the lemonade stand. Jack, seventy-eight, retired in 2017 after a long career, most recently leading the pension management business for State Street Bank. He has white-flecked brown hair and a quiet, friendly demeanor that invites conversation.

I asked Jack if his life in finance influenced his son's decision to pursue a career in accounting. "He actually had two influencers," Jack said. "My father was an Arthur Andersen partner and was very supportive of Ryan when he was growing up, and particularly when he decided to go to Georgetown and major in accounting." One of the best lessons Ryan learned at Georgetown happened not through his classes, but how they were paid for. Jack provided Ryan with a set amount of cash to pay for his education, room, and board. Ryan could have chosen to attend a lower-cost school, graduate in four years, and buy a car, but instead he chose to attend Georgetown and graduate in three years to stay within his budget. "It helps to have some skin in the game," Jack said.

What advice did Jack have for teaching finance to the next generation? "From an investing standpoint, you should not count on anyone else to take care of you," he said. "Which means that as soon as you start working you have to be putting away money for retirement and contingencies. Think long-term about your money, and don't spend it unless you have it." Jack's thrifty Midwest family life instilled in him, and his son (and ultimately the grandsons we have in common), a love of saving, avoidance of debt, and a dedication to charitable giving. "From a very young age," Jack said, "I had to manage my allowance: 10 percent should go into savings, 10 percent goes in the basket at church on Sunday, and the rest is yours to spend, in that order."

Talking about debt compelled me to ask Jack what he thought about how our government spends money. "I think it's a travesty," he said. "Initially, the idea was that government could go into debt to help stabilize the economy. But when the economy was good they'd collect our taxes and pay off the debt, and so we'd build a surplus for the next time there was a problem. But it's gotten so we spend just as much or more in good times and we're not paying off the debt. We're mortgaging our children's future."

I asked Jack for the number one thing. "Life isn't just about you," Jack said. "I'd say treat others better than you expect to be treated. What I mean by that is that others aren't necessarily going to do that. It's kind of dog eat dog, right? So, you need to go beyond the Golden Rule. Treat them *better*."

There will be a time in our grandchildren's lives to instill this brand of thoughtful wisdom. In the meantime, we have lemonade. If there is a heaven—and I strongly suspect there is—Gramp smiled at the sight of his great-grandsons jumping up and down with excitement at their profitable and charitable roadside venture, their whole lives ahead of them. "That's just dandy," he said. "Wonderful!"

CHAPTER 13

A Lab of Their Own

Try as we might as parents, we all know that it can be impossible to get our offspring to follow in our footsteps. My dad strongly encouraged me and my brothers to love science as much as he did. He put his master's in chemical engineering to work at home by turning a room in our basement into a full lab complete with vials of chemical compounds and a Bunsen burner. My eldest brother, Calvin, spent the most time in the lab, but what he did there could have gotten us all killed; his homemade pipe bombs were rudimentary but ingenious devices that packed a wallop far bigger than any M-80 firecracker. He even created timing mechanisms for his bombs, retrofit from the heads of parking meters he sawed off in downtown Lexington. For many years, parking in our town was virtually free thanks to Calvin. One of these bombs, timed to go off during a family dinner, blew a three-foot hole in the side of our playhouse in the backyard.

When Calvin was in high school, he bought an industrial blowtorch to make metal sculptures for art class, an endeavor my parents applauded. Little did they know that Calvin would combine the two gasses from his blowtorch—oxygen and acetylene—into a balloon that, when suspended over a candle at my birthday party, created a shocking boom and fireball that rivaled Hiroshima. My friends ran screaming from the yard, and the police arrived minutes later. As adults, my parents, brothers, and I worried that Calvin was the Unabomber. We were very relieved when the Unabomber's brother turned him in, because it meant we didn't have to.

Never one to give up on a project, my dad turned to me as another opportunity to instill the love of science. This did not go well. Dad gave me a large magnifying glass when I was in the third grade. I marveled at its ability to make the tiny universe large, turning ants into dinosaurs. I was delighted to see one day in class that by holding the magnifying glass at just the right angle I could focus sunlight into a small, intensely bright circle on the canvas sneaker of the boy in front of me. A plume of smoke soon rose from the white dot, nearly setting the sneaker ablaze. I got into a lot of trouble. "Why all the fuss?" I could have protested while sulking in the principal's office. "I was simply applying science to advance human understanding!"

For my mom, the fact that we were causing trouble was not nearly as concerning as the reality that everyone in the house had a penis except for her. She longed to have a girl, just one, to make dresses for and do other feminine things. As child number five I was her last try to have a girl, but it was not to be. After I was born, she gave up and got a female dog. Even with another girl in the house, though, Mom complained about the dominance of males, especially after she joined NOW, the National Organization for Women, in the 1970s. Attending NOW conferences gave her a chance to vent with other like-minded women, which unfortunately brought zero change to how the house was overrun by males. As kids, we never questioned how our father was able to arrive home every weeknight exactly at 6:30 to sit down for the dinner Mom had prepared, regardless of how heavy the Cambridge traffic was. It wasn't until years later that we learned that Dad always stopped at the Lexington library on his way home. He'd pick up and drop off books and leave the library at precisely 6:27 so he could stroll into the kitchen after all the work was done. No wonder Mom was pissed off.

Not every family had the same experience. Five years after I was born, a girl was born a world away in Hawaii. She was very bright and excelled in her studies, particularly science. She was also fortunate to have both a father and mother who fully supported her love of all things scientific. In high school, the girl told her guidance counselor she wanted to focus on science when she went to college and asked him for advice on the best schools to apply to. His response was, "Science is for men."

If you've read Walter Isaacson's excellent book *The Code Breaker*, you'll now that the girl's name was Jennifer Doudna. To the great benefit of humanity, Jennifer had a strong spine and would not allow anyone to crush her ambitions. She not only majored in science, she earned a PhD and eventually co-invented CRISPR gene-editing technology, birthing a revolution in medicine. In 2020, Jennifer shared the Nobel Prize in chemistry. I'll return to her work later in this chapter.

I relate these stories to tee up some important questions: How can we make sure that no girl is ever, *ever* told by a man to limit her dreams? And how can we help kick open doors of possibility for both boys and girls alike? For me, this is personal. I have three granddaughters and two grandsons. For them to be part of the greatest of all generations, they must have an equal playing field.

Women have made progress in our society, but there's still a long and arduous road ahead for our granddaughters. Women represent about half of the US workforce, yet only 27 percent are STEM workers (science, technology, engineering, math).[8] One reason for this might be that women are still being discouraged and discriminated against when it comes to science and technology. And there is evidence that even when women do go into scientific fields, there are hurdles to recognition. A study published in *Nature* states that "women in research teams are significantly less likely than men to be credited with authorship."

The hard truth is that we grandparents have lived our entire lives and careers in a world where women are, in a word, less. I witnessed this in my first job in advertising when I was with the McCann Erickson ad agency in New York City. McCann was, and remains, one of the largest ad agencies in the world. If you've ever seen the TV show *Mad Men* you'll get a sense of what it was like to work in advertising in those days. Most of the people in our creative department, and in fact the entire agency, were men. The one shining exception was our executive creative director, Nina DiSesa. She was awesome. Nina would stride into our *Mad Men* meetings with an air of total confidence, her long cowgirl dress billowing behind her, and either crush an ad concept to death with her high-heeled cowboy boots or praise it to the moon and back, and either way I knew she was right. Nina, however, was definitely the rare female exception in the McCann penis-dominated conglomerate. I may have been working in a Midtown skyscraper, but it was basically the same kind of house that I grew up in, minus the bombs.

Six months into my tenure at McCann, as my bosses saw my star rising, I was given a window office with a magnificent view of the Chrysler Building. I had arrived. My departure, however, was imminent. A woman in the creative department who had been with the company longer than me complained that she was first in line for the window office. Within a week of her complaint my bosses apologized to her (and to me, quietly), and I sulked back to my cubicle. At the time, I had mixed feelings about it. On the one hand, I felt I was worthy of a promotion and a better office. On the other hand, my female cohort was no doubt equally deserving *and* she'd been there longer. I shrugged my shoulders and moved on. Today, I see the woman who took the window office as someone's granddaughter.

We can't go back in time to redress the wrongs of the past. All we have is our future, these grandkids together with us. I've come to the conclusion that there is no single solution but rather a host of things that can be done in tandem that will allow our grandgirls to rise. It's complicated. So, I suggest we start with the simplest thing, something grandparents are very good at: playing.

My granddaughters are lucky to have two grandpas and two grandmas. My daughter-in-law's parents, Jill and Roy Levian, spend a lot of time with our granddaughters, babysitting and playing in ways that put their young minds to work. The concept of baby*sitting* doesn't capture the sheer volume of activity involved in being with these girls, who as of this writing are all under five years of age. Our shared granddaughters are fast-moving dust storms of glitter, whirling dervishes of spinning rainbow kitty dresses, fearless rock wall climbing adventurers, the girls on the swings who ask to be pushed higher and higher. Simply observing these girls can be exhausting, but we grandparents do activities with them, too, because it's fun, and because the girls love having us along for the ride. We also give them different kinds of toys to play with.

That's how I found myself one day at my son's house sitting at a long table with my granddaughters, thinking about our next activity. The five-year-old, Roen, looked at me with her big brown eyes and asked, "Let's do an experiment!" I said, "Sure!" And before I knew it the girls had brought out a science kit that Roy and Jill had given them, complete with little test tubes and vials of fluid. I felt like I was right back in my childhood chemistry lab, only now it was a little girl at the lab bench—perhaps our future Madame Curie—diving with gusto into a world of scientific discovery. I read the instructions and the girls measured out the fluids and mixed them together. They were delighted to see the color of the fluid in the vial change as new compounds were added and mixed, and thrilled to discover the result: a pink rose petal perfume. They took turns sniffing the sweet aroma they had created, their Chanel No. 5, and laughed as they dabbed some on their wrists. Pure magic.

This kind of playtime matters a lot. The choice of toys matters, too. Jenna Connolly asked in her TED Talk, "Do the toys our girls play with today determine their future tomorrow?" The answer is an emphatic *yes*. Her research revealed that in the early part of the twentieth century, boys typically wore pink clothes, and girls wore blue. After World War II, Rosie the Riveter turned in her blue overalls and, under the influence of my Madison Avenue peers, switched to pink. Toy shelves became stocked with pink toys for girls and blue toys for boys. But they were different kinds of toys. The pink girl toys were things like kitchen playsets, the boy's toys more often mechanical in nature, like construction sets. The boy toys enabled better learning of spatial intelligence skills—central to what's needed for careers in science and engineering.

I should point out here that my granddaughters are absolutely bonkers about Disney-themed clothes and dolls. Their favorite Disney character, bar none, is Elsa from the movie *Frozen*. But take a close look at Elsa and you'll see characteristics that show exactly why my grandgirls aspire to be like her. Elsa is powerful. Anything she touches freezes solid. And the color of her dress? It's blue. My grandgirls may be feminine to the max, but trust me on this: they are in charge. Watch out, world.

I'll tell you a brief story to illustrate exactly what can happen when women in science are in charge and why it matters so much, both for us and our grandkids.

It was the height of the COVID-19 mania. The pandemic had been tough for everybody, but especially for grandparents. Not only did the illness cause more deaths among older age groups, it also built a wall between the generations just when everyone needed their loved ones the most. For my wife and me, being apart from our children and grandchildren felt like being exiled to a foreign land. Playground romps and bedtime books were replaced by rations of Zoom and FaceTime. It's not that the video chats were infrequent; we were jumping on the phone multiple times every week, often daily. But too often our calls seemed like reminders that we could not really be there with our grandkids. And all the while we knew they were growing up without us. That was painful. Still, we reminded ourselves that our parents' generation had it a lot worse; they lived through the Great Depression and a horrific world war. Surely we could manage through the masks and isolation. Job one was simply to stay alive. Which meant staying alone.

This began to change one day in March of 2022 when I experienced an unexpected chorus. I'd gone to get my first shot of the Pfizer vaccine—one developed using Jennifer Doudna's CRISPR gene-editing technology. For months I'd seen the absolute misery and pain of front-line health-care workers struggling to help COVID patients in the face of short supplies and overwhelming caseloads. But in the hall that day a different mood prevailed. The space was suffused with hope and happiness, and while I could not see the smiles behind the masks of the nurses, their eyes spoke volumes. At last, here was something positive they could do.

After the quick jab, I sat in the hall for the required half hour. And it was there, as I thumbed through emails, that a song welled up on the loudspeakers. It was Bill Withers singing "Lean On Me." Quiet at first, then building as one by one, like a wave, the nurses, volunteers, and patients started to sing along. Behind the big sheets of plexiglass the nurses sang and swayed to the music, this rapidly growing chorus of those who had been beat down but were now rising, together. I sang, too. It was an electric feeling.

Within a few months, the second vaccine shot behind us, my wife and I were finally able to see our children and grandchildren again. There were many hugs and tears. I hoisted one of my grandgirls in the air and carried her on my shoulders. I chased my grandsons through playgrounds, the Tickle Monster again. I met our newest grandbaby for the first time.

In a way, our grandchildren seemed the same (although bigger). But when my oldest grandson grabbed a book so we could read together, it was now him proudly reading to me. The gap of time we'd lost together was suddenly palpable. This made me sad, yet I was also happy—filled with joy, actually—because despite the many challenges of the past year our family had continued to grow and persevere. Our bonds had become even stronger. And once again, with the love of all those around me, I knew I could be there for them.

My family and I, and millions of others, survived because a girl persisted. Today, the greatest generation of all is waiting in the wings, boys and girls, ready to take center stage to invent an amazing world. If we grandparents give them our support—someone to lean on—we'll have done our job.

CHAPTER 14

The Six Grandfathers

In 1966, when I was seven years old, my dad decided it was time for us to take a road trip so my brothers and I could experience firsthand the hopeful America he'd written about in his letter to us in 1956. He retrofit a big white van with a wooden cargo hold in the center of the passenger area, which allowed enough room for luggage but definitely not enough room for five large boys and two parents. We were joined at the hip for seemingly endless miles from Massachusetts into the western states, stopping along the way at Holiday Inns. The shimmering green aura of the motels felt to me like the land of Oz.

When we got to South Dakota, Mom and Dad bought all of us white cowboy hats. I was living a John Wayne cowboy dream, my eyes wide open to the wonders of the Badlands and their broad, wide-open skies, so different from New England. Visiting this region of South Dakota was no mere side trip. As I was soon to discover, there was meaning embedded in the hills that Dad wanted us to know about as we embarked on our young

American lives. Specifically, a string of famous mountain peaks. One day we left Oz, piled into the van with our cowboy hats, and headed out for our learning experience. I recall distinctly the moment I saw the mountains before me. Majestic. Magnificent. Craggy. Mysterious. I held my mother's hand; my jaw dropped.

"This," my father said, beaming, "is the Six Grandfathers."

We joined a group of other tourists who'd gathered around a park ranger as he told us the story of the Grandfathers. These six peaks, he explained, were an ancient sacred place of the Lakota Sioux tribe, the source of the treasured teachings they passed on from one generation to the next. Each of the towering six peaks held a different meaning.[9]

The first grandfather is known as Mato Tipila, meaning Bear Lodge, symbolizing wisdom and knowledge.

To the east of Bear Lodge is Mato Paha, Bear Mountain, representing strength and fortitude.

Next is Mato Kheya, Wolf Mountain, which symbolizes bravery, its rocky face and lines conveying the courage and fearlessness required to confront adversity.

Skan Skan, White Crow, is next, representing the compassion and generosity essential for supporting communities.

Shoulder to shoulder with Mato Kheya stands Hinhan Kaga, Thunderhead Mountain. It stands for respect—for others, oneself, and the world of nature.

Last but not least is a majestic peak called Wamblie Luta, Eagle Nest Mountain. Its wings soar above to signal respect for love and spirituality.

Even to my six-year-old self, it was amazing to learn that so much meaning could be embedded in a place.

Except, this is not exactly what I experienced that day.

We did visit a national park, and we did look up at an awe-inspiring mountain ridge, but it was Mount Rushmore. The park was crowded with tourists like us who had come to see the iconic faces of Presidents Washington, Lincoln, Roosevelt, and Jefferson carved in stone. I learned a lot about Mount Rushmore that day, but I did not learn that this same mountain was a sacred Native American site—one that was, in their view, desecrated by white invaders when the sculpture was created. I didn't learn this until a few weeks ago when I googled "South Dakota Grandfather." When I read about it, I smacked my palm against my forehead and said out loud, "How did I not know this?!"

It's not like I'm uneducated. I studied American history in high school. But, of course, the reason I've been ignorant all this time is because the story of the Six Grandfathers of South Dakota was not taught in my schools. The Native American ancestry of the Six Grandfathers has largely been whitewashed. To be fair, the National Park Service now has a Lakota, Nakota, and Dakota Heritage Village at Mount Rushmore where visitors can learn about Native American culture and history. This was a long time coming, however, and I strongly doubt the story of the Six Grandfathers is taught in most schools even today.

I did more digging and learned that one of the presidents carved on the rock face, Theodore Roosevelt—the man I was named after—once said, "I don't go so far as to think that the only good Indians are the dead Indians, but I believe nine out of every ten are, and I shouldn't like to inquire too closely into the case of the tenth." Process this for one moment: the US broke a treaty with the Lakota Sioux for the Black Hills land after gold was discovered there, then we carved up the Lakotas' sacred mountain with the face of a president who wanted them all dead. And this place has become one of the most iconic meccas of our American republic. I should mention that I'm no fan of cancel culture. Some people in Britain have argued for the removal of statues of Winston Churchill, an avowed imperialist.

This despite the reality that if not for Churchill, the official language of the United Kingdom today would be German. But in South Dakota and many other places, it is the Native Americans who were canceled.

Learning one part of the story of the Six Grandfathers drove me to learn more, and to unpack their meaning on a deeper level—especially focusing on Native American perspectives on the value of society's elders. It's fascinating to contrast the sacredness of the Six Grandfathers with how grandfathers have been portrayed in American and European cultures. As just one recent example, Europe's two-ton ERS spacecraft, which had played a leading role in analyzing Earth's atmosphere for many years, burned up over the Pacific Ocean in February of 2024. It stopped working in 2011 (one could say it retired after a long career), and what do you suppose the space agencies named it when it fell to Earth? They called it the Grandfather Satellite. What does this say about how people view grandfathers? It's the science version of the movie *Bad Grandpa.* Nobody is going to hold a spirit dance at the place where the burnt shards of the Grandfather Satellite fell into the Pacific, that vast aquatic nursing home. It's ironic that one of the key things the ERS spacecraft helped measure was climate change. We apply humanity's prodigious technical advancements toward determining how our planet's atmosphere is changing, but nothing to measure how our culture is changing for the worse here on the ground.

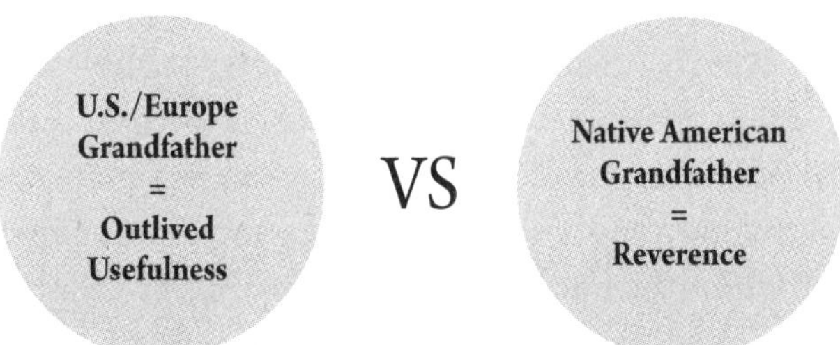

In my native New England, we have our own majestic peaks. The White Mountains in New Hampshire are stunning. But just as Mount Rushmore features American presidents, the White Mountains are known for their Presidential Range, comprised of mountains named after presidents such as Washington, Jefferson, Adams, Madison, and Monroe. Even a natural rock formation in New Hampshire's Franconia Notch that formed a gigantic face in profile was named the Old Man of the Mountain, not the Grandfather. There are plenty of good grandpas in New Hampshire, but they ain't sacred peaks.

In Robin Wall Kimmerer's gorgeous book *Braiding Sweetgrass*, she weaves together stories of rediscovering her Native American roots and language with a thoughtful perspective that reveals something the ERS spacecraft could never see: the inextricable connection between the science of botany and the deep spirituality of nature in all its forms. Kimmerer describes sitting in a forest and listening. Listening intently to the songs of birds, the soft buzz of insects, the wind in the trees. All living things, from animals to the copious green alga she raked from her pond to make it swimmable for her daughters, are portrayed with a sense of reverence. She also relates stories told by her grandfather about when he was a boy in upstate New York. Reading her book (slowly to savor every page), it struck me that listening to nature, and listening to our elders, are the same thing. So much of the richness and wonder of our world has been passed down from generation to generation. The old maple trees on my Vermont farm exist because of their ancestors, and they are—as Robin points out in her book—connected through their root systems with other trees in a communicative and mutually supportive community. If we look and listen carefully in a forest, we can learn from them just as much as we can learn from elders like my aunt Lois, or my Gram and Gramp, or yours.

Bearing all this in mind, it's nevertheless vital for us as Americans to understand why we have so much reverence for the presidents sculpted in South Dakota or dotting our New England ridgelines. We should not erase history but rather take from it the lessons most valuable for us today, and for future generations. I believe the sacred Six Grandfathers of the Lakota are still there at Mount Rushmore, if we only choose to learn about them and celebrate their meaning. Something so powerful cannot be removed by a chisel. Four of America's most exceptional presidents have been overlaid on top, each with its own meaning for our country and the world. This, perhaps, is the essence of what America is all about—despite our many faults and the injustices done to the Native Americans. All we have is the future. We can't go back. Waves of new people arrive and bring something different, and we join together, layer upon layer, and through this interconnection we are forged into something new and—at our best—exceptional.

As a thought experiment, here is the meaning of each of the presidents of Mount Rushmore, overlayed with the sacred meanings of the Six Grandfathers.

George Washington: Freedom. More than any other Founding Father, he represents the fight for liberty in the face of tyranny.

Abraham Lincoln: Righteous justice. As the president who freed the slaves, he represents the everlasting truth that all men and women are created equal.

Theodore Roosevelt: Grit. Teddy fought for progressive causes and broke up powerful corporate trusts. And he nearly died leading an expedition into the Amazon after leaving office, when others were content to read books at the seashore.

Thomas Jefferson: 360° learning. Jefferson was a polymath who constantly delved into new areas of discovery. President John F. Kennedy hosted a dinner at the White House for

> leading thinkers and Nobel laureates. He said, "I think this is the most extraordinary collection of talent, of human knowledge, that has ever been gathered together at the White House, with the possible exception of when Thomas Jefferson dined alone."

When we add the meaning of the presidents to the meaning of the Six Grandfathers, we can see a broader and more multidimensional view of America.

Mato Tipila Wisdom & Knowledge	**Mato Paha** Strength & Fortitude	**Mato Kheya** Bravery	**Skan Skan** Compassion & Generosity	**Hinhan Kaga** Respect	**Wamblie Luta** Love & Spirituality
Washington Freedom	**Lincoln** Righteous Justice	**Roosevelt** Grit	**Jefferson** 360° Learning		

This landscape of American meaning reminds me of what grandpa Fred Schoch shared with me when I asked him for his essential wisdom: a desire to convey the basic building blocks of what it means to be a decent human being. I set out with this book to find *new* ways to help our grandchildren live their best lives. Yet what I'm finding is that *it's the old things that matter most,* like our ancient mountains, our Founding Fathers, and the wisdom of the elderly among us. We can't look down to find these things, as in the swamp of cable news where disagreements become intractable conflicts as entertainment. We and our grandchildren must look up. What Lincoln called the "better angels of our nature" are there before us rising high toward the big sky, if we can only make the choice to see.

Putting this philosophy into practice today as a grandpa is not easy. I honestly wrestle with it—too often my better angels can't take off at all, let alone fly. But once in a while I see something that lifts me up unexpectedly. This happened recently when we were with our daughter and her family for Thanksgiving, and Mr. Ted Laws (another Theodore) and his wife joined us for dinner. Their son, Alex, is a good friend of my son-in-law, and their family has become a welcome extension to ours at our traditional turkey day feast. Before dinner, we always go around the table and say what we are most thankful for. At this particular dinner, one by one we shared our thanks for things like our loved ones, the beautiful house, and wonderful food.

Finally, after everyone else had weighed in, it was Ted Laws's turn. Ted is many years my senior—nearly eighty—old enough to seem like he's from a different generation than mine. His face is deeply lined (not unlike the crevices of a rock cliff, a cloud of white hair floating above). Ted looked down at his plate, collecting his thoughts. Many seconds passed, and still more before I realized he was trying to control his emotions. Then he said, "I'm so thankful we live in this great country of ours. I'm thankful for our first responders, our police, our firefighters, and our veterans. We are truly blessed." Something clicked in my mind just then, an "aha" moment. I and everyone else had showed thanks for *what we had*. Ted's thanks were for *the things that made it possible for us to have those things.*

Ted looked up and smiled. Our grandsons nodded thoughtfully. We said, "Amen."

CHAPTER 15

The World Next Door

At dusk on a cool June day in 1969, the fireflies began blinking on and off as they flew over a Vermont meadow of waving grass. The darker the sky became, the brighter the fireflies seemed, their light creating tracers of yellow sparks that bobbed and weaved, and before long the stars came out, too, completing the light show. Ten years old at the time, I'd seen the beautiful flight of the fireflies many times, but on this night I—along with my cousin Sara, eleven, and my brother John, fourteen—decided to try something new. We each took an old glass jar from the house, punched holes in the metal lids, and had a contest to see who could capture the most fireflies. I chased one intermittent spark after another, holding up my jar to scoop up the fireflies one by one, and before long I made an unexpected discovery. Dozens of fireflies in a jar added up to a glowing lantern. The fireflies were too numerous to count, so we agreed we had all won the contest and set them free, waving and spinning the open jars to unleash a shower of blinking sparks around us.

On the other side of the world on Mount Abu in Rajasthan, India, a boy my age in that same year was playing in a lush forest with his cousins. Dark green moss coated the trunks of subtropical evergreens and mango trees, and here and there purple orchids rose up in the mist to catch gleams of light. Through gaps in the tree limbs they could glimpse the arid plains below. The boy came across a beehive and set to work building a smoky fire beneath it to drive away the bees, then wrapped the hive in a handkerchief and squeezed the honey into his mouth. The boy's name was Saif (pronounced Safe). Recently, Saif—now a grandfather—joined me in my living room in Lexington to talk about his life experiences.

How a child of Mount Abu came to be in my house in a historic Boston suburb is a story in itself. The unofficial tagline for Lexington is "The Birthplace of the American Revolution." The first shot of the battle for independence was fired here on the town green on April 19, 1775, and every year they hold a reenactment of the battle. One of my ancestors, Lemuel Page, was a fifer in George Washington's army (it figures a Page would be the musician). Back in the '60s when I was growing up here, Lexington was basically all white. In recent decades there's been a welcome influx of Asian Americans. In fact, approximately 30 percent of the population today is Asian, mostly Chinese and Indian. So, when I sought out an Indian grandpa to meet with, all I needed to do was walk across the street and introduce myself. Two years ago, a young couple had moved in, Jason and Zayneb, along with their infant daughter, Alia. Zayneb is originally from New Delhi. For about six months each year, Zayneb's parents live with them so they can spend more time with Alia.

My goal in talking with Saif was to gain a more global view of grandfatherhood. After all, the concept of nurturing the next great generation should apply to *all* grandchildren in every country. I was also curious to learn about cultural differences that might inform new pathways to understanding.

Saif is about five foot seven, with white streaks in his dark hair and a neatly trimmed white beard. We started our conversation at the beginning, where I learned that he was born the same year as me, 1959, and raised in a small town in the state of Gujarat. He spent much of his childhood attending Saint Mary's High School at Mount Abu, where he was taught by an Irish priest. "We call Mount Abu a hill station," Saif explained, "because it's not at sea level. Most of India has a hot climate throughout the year, but at the higher elevations it's much cooler." Saif's family had a house nearby where his entire extended family lived—parents, cousins, grandparents. "We would all interact and bond with each other," Saif said. "We played cricket together." It was usually Saif's cousin's grandmother who looked after him, a woman he described as extremely strict. "I was beaten up a lot," he said, admitting wryly, "I was a very naughty boy." Saif's dad and grandfather had a prosperous business that imported yarn and special fabrics, mostly from Japan, which they sold in New Delhi. Mentored by his elders in the world of fabrics, Saif was inspired to start his own custom-tailoring business. Today, he's semiretired so he can spend more time with his grandchildren and enjoy life.

When I asked Saif about Indian culture, I learned that there is actually no such thing, or rather no singular culture that could define something so varied. "India is a vast country," Saif said. "Every state has practically its own language. You have different religions, different festivals, different dances. I mean, it's like a cohesion of all these people together." Hearing this made me think of the United States and how different South Carolina is from Vermont, or Texas from Maine. We don't necessarily have our own languages and dialects, but that doesn't make it any easier for us to understand each other. India is on a whole different level.

In India, even the words used to describe grandfathers and grandmothers are different depending on family lineage. "We call a paternal grandfather and maternal grandfather by different names," Saif explained. "The same with grandmothers. They call me Nana because I'm the maternal grandfather. If I was the paternal grandfather, I'd be Dada." Being the Nana or Dada matters in India when it comes to the degree of closeness to grandchildren. "In India, generally, maternal grandparents are closer to the grandchildren than the paternal grandparents," Saif explained. This difference is relevant for Saif because as the Nana he's able to spend a lot more time with his granddaughter. If he'd been the paternal grandfather, this scenario would be unlikely.

Saif and his wife play different roles as grandparents. "Alia likes to play make-believe, with a doll or whatever, but I prefer to play more with a physical toy like a puzzle and take her out for biking in the park." Saif's wife is more active in the realm of make-believe and does the cooking.

Upon hearing Saif's tales of Indian life and culture, I suddenly pictured a huge family wedding dance scene in a Bollywood movie, which now included me—a very tall Nana Ted—in the middle of a kick line. I told Saif that if I ever go to India I may never return. I'll just wander up the Ganges and settle down in a village near the Himalayas, where I'll join a cricket team and meditate.

When the conversation turned to how we could help our grandkids become the greatest of all generations, Saif surprised me. "They already are," he said, "one hundred percent. It goes without saying. I grew up in a very small town. There was no TV. No movie theater whatsoever. There were no opportunities at all, other than we found life wonderful."

Within the context of the history of India and other developing countries, Saif's perspective makes perfect sense. Since 1990, child mortality rates globally have been cut by more than half thanks to improvements in sanitation and health care.[10] In the 1960s, when Saif and I were boys, the poverty rate in India was as high as 54 percent.[11] By 2023 that had dropped to around 4.5 percent.[12] In 1950, only two out of every ten Indians were literate.[13] As of 2022, the literacy rate nationally was over 76 percent[14] and climbing fast (some estimates are considerably higher). For us Americans, the mythology of the greatest generation was largely created around our victory in World War II. What the people of India are achieving today is a victory over poverty and illiteracy; they are kicking open the doors of opportunity on the global stage.

That said, Saif sees room for improvement for our grandchildren. "When we were children we were satisfied with what we had," he said. "Today it's become more materialistic—'I want this. I want this. I want this.'" Saif also sees a contrast between the close family bonds forged in his childhood and today's dispersed nuclear families, not to mention the challenges of incessant screen time. He sees too many families plopping kids in front of TVs and "shoveling food in their mouths. We never do that. With Alia, there's half an hour of screen time per day. That's it!"

When I asked Saif for his number one piece of wisdom for the next generation, he said, "The main thing is, we want to inculcate a sense of gratitude. Be thankful, and also believe in a higher power." This wisdom is deeply grounded in Saif's Muslim faith. Saif and his wife roll out their prayer mats five times each day. When Alia asks why they are praying, the answer is, "We are thankful for spending time with you. We are thankful we have everything, and God has given us such lovely grandchildren, and you have got such lovely parents." Saif went on to explain that even though his grandchildren are not being raised Muslim, having a sense of gratitude and a belief in a higher power are essentially the same thing. You can't really have one without the other. I was reminded that we grandfathers in 2024, we Nanas and Dadas, are part of a larger spiritual heritage that goes back to the earliest days of religion. The prophet Muhammad was a grandfather.

I thought what Saif shared with me was beautiful and valuable on so many levels. We have great wealth, poverty, and everything in between in the US—but how much gratitude do we really feel for whatever we have now? Not enough. There is so much abundance it creates a blur, a white noise, that blots out our ability to appreciate our many gifts. When my wife and I go Halloween trick-or-treating with our grandkids and they're given candy at each door, we have to keep repeating, "What do you say?" Only then do they say, "Thank you!"

One area where I think we lack a sense of gratitude is in regards to our freedom. It's taken for granted that we can speak our minds. This is guaranteed by our Constitution. We may fight like dogs with people who support other political candidates, but this, too, is freedom. When we're done fighting we go to the same football games together. We've been free for so long in this country we've forgotten what it truly means. We can stand on a Facebook soapbox and say whatever we please about the president of the United States, and he or she can't exile us to a freezing Siberian prison cell. I don't have the answers to how we can instill a greater sense of gratitude for ourselves and our grandchildren, but I believe in my heart that Saif is right that we must try.

* * *

Around the time Saif was squeezing honey from the beehives on Mount Abu, a five-year-old boy named Jun Zhao in the Chinese city of Tianjin made a very exciting discovery. He'd always been very eager to learn, so when he found out the local grade school had an opening he literally jumped out of his tub, ran naked through the crowded city streets to the school, and demanded, "Teach me!" The only problem was that he had to be six years old to enroll. Unbowed, he ran home and rolled and kicked on the floor until his parents agreed to help him get in.

I was delighted to meet up with Jun, along with his daughter, who provided translation, where I learned that his childhood sprint through the streets of Tianjin was only the beginning of a decades-long quest to gain knowledge, a quest that took place amid the hardships and repressive turmoil of the Cultural Revolution. Jun, now a proud grandpa, has black hair streaked with white and a friendly, open demeanor that made me feel right at home despite our different languages.

The Chinese economy of Jun's youth offered little in the way of opportunities. Jun's father was a truck driver who worked most of the year in a different city, providing a meager paycheck that was stretched thin. Jun and his four siblings, along with his mother and grandmother, all lived in one apartment, often going hungry for lack of food. A good meal—which was all too rare—was comprised of rice with some sweet potatoes mixed in. Jun loved to draw from a very young age, but there was no money for luxuries like paper and paint, so he used chalk to draw on the back of a door.

Jun did finally manage to gain entrance to his local grade school, but his insatiable hunger for learning was stymied yet again when he was in fourth grade. The Cultural Revolution exploded, sending shock waves of upheaval across the country. All the schools were closed. Worse, Jun's family—due to an arbitrary judgment by the communist regime—was designated as belonging to one of the Five Black Categories. People lumped into these categories, like landlords and rich farmers, were considered enemies of the revolution.

When I heard this I shook my head. How on earth, I wondered, could a truck driver and his poor family be somehow considered contemptable, as if they were the much-maligned bourgeoisie intellectuals that Mao railed against? The sheer randomness of it all struck me as bizarre, but such was life under the communists. It got worse. In 1968, Mao launched the Down to the Countryside Movement, where young people living in cities were ordered to move to rural areas to work on farms. Life was very hard.

Finally, in 1972, Jun was allowed to go back to the city, where he jumped at the chance to return to school. He hadn't been able to attend middle school, but because of his age he was allowed to enroll directly in high school. To get caught up on everything he missed in middle school he borrowed his younger brother's notebooks and studied them at night. He excelled in his studies and graduated at the top of his class. Despite his excellent grades, however, the regime would not allow him to go to college. He landed an art teaching gig with a local grade school, supplementing his income by painting murals showing a beaming Chairman Mao with "inspiring" slogans. The irony of being hired to paint propaganda of the dictator who was persecuting his family was not lost on me.

Not until 1977, one year after Mao died, was Jun allowed to take a test where he could qualify to enter college. After over a decade where so few young people were allowed to attend college, there was tremendous pent-up demand for a limited number of slots. Jun learned to his alarm that out of one hundred openings, only three students would be selected. And he had only a few months to cram for the exam. Nothing was going to stand in his way. Jun burned the midnight oil and made it happen. After graduation, he became a successful manager for a manufacturing company, rising in the ranks to become a vice president before retiring in 2018.

Today, Jun and his wife live with their daughter, Mei, and young granddaughter in the US for half the year. Given the closeness of their relationship, I wanted to hear his daughter's perspectives on their lives together. I asked what brought her to the US and about the role her grandparents play in the upbringing of her daughter. Mei graduated from college in China before going to grad school here, focusing on scientific research. She decided to stay. "I feel like in my case the culture here is more open," Mei said. "In China, it's more rigid, like layers of hierarchy in a company or school. In grad school, it's like we were more equal. We could discuss my thinking and proposals. In China, I'd have to do whatever they ordered me to do."

When it comes to taking care of her young daughter, Mei and her parents have established clear lanes, all with a solid grounding in respect and admiration. "Chinese people, we feel like we want to spend time with the grandparents because that's our wealth from our culture," Mei said. "We really appreciate that time with my parents. They also can help us for a little bit, like cook for us. But we don't consider them a primary educator. I told him, 'Education is our responsibility. Just love my kids.'"

I asked Jun how our grandchildren could be nurtured to become the greatest generation of all time. Whenever I meet grandpas and ask this question, I never know what to expect. Or, to be more accurate, I've learned to expect anything. But what Jun and Mei shared with me at that moment was nevertheless unexpected and really wonderful. Jun brought out some of his paintings and laid them across the table—beautiful paintings with fine brush strokes and gorgeous details, a peacock with brightly colored feathers in its flowing tail, a glowing sunset over a rural Chinese village, and much more. "My father says he tries to introduce Chinese culture to my daughter," Mei said. "He teaches her to hold a brush, how to paint." To celebrate Chinese New Year, Jun and his granddaughter collaborated to paint festive decorations to put around their front door, with words painted in white against a bright red background. Jun had written traditional Chinese good wishes, like, "May more wealth come to this house." His granddaughter's contribution, boldly displayed above the door, read, "I love my cat."

I asked Jun for his number one thing. After all his striving to earn a great education, his many years in the work world, and his time as a parent and a grandparent, what was the essential wisdom he'd want to share with his grandchildren? "Be kind," he replied immediately in Chinese. "I try to teach my granddaughter to be nice around her friends. That's the most important thing."

Before we parted ways, Jun gave me one of his beautiful paintings—a panda playing in a bamboo tree, swinging from a branch. I will always cherish it.

Just down the road from my house, not far from the town green where the colonial militia fought their first battle with the British, there is an old train station that's been turned into the Lexington Historical Society building. Each year on the fifteenth day of the first month of the lunar calendar on the full moon, the town celebrates with a Lantern Festival organized by the thriving Chinese American community here. During the Han dynasty, this date was significant. People started celebrating it to honor Buddha. Today, its larger purpose is to promote reconciliation, peace, and forgiveness. Brilliantly colored Chinese lanterns of every size, glowing as if filled with a thousand fireflies, are held aloft by adults and children alike. Students of

American history will recall that Paul Revere arranged to have a signal lit in the Old North Church in Boston to let the surrounding towns know how the invading British forces would arrive—one lantern if by land, two if by sea. The Chinese lanterns that gleam in our historic district are a vivid reminder of the iridescence of freedom, the love of family, the light of learning, and the beauty of embracing all cultures with open arms.

A few weeks ago on an early spring day, my wife and I were babysitting our granddaughters and decided we'd plant some sunflower seeds together as an activity. We invited Alia over so she could join us around the table on our patio where we laid out pods of soil and packets of sunflower seeds. We showed them how to push the seeds down into the soil with their fingers, and they took turns with the watering to get the soil good and moist. They listened as we talked about how the seeds would need plant food, regular watering, and sunlight most of all. We, and they, can't wait to see what will grow.

CHAPTER 16

Grandma's Karmann Ghia

On December 3, 1947, the blond-coiffed professional wrestler known as Gorgeous George ascended into the ring of the Olympic Auditorium in Los Angeles, basking in the applause and jeers of the massive crowd. He was joined in the ring by his opponent, a six-foot-tall, muscular Black wrestler who went by the name of Reginald Siki, sometimes called the Panther. The instant the starting bell rang, George ran at Siki, took a flying leap, and delivered a dropkick to his chin. Siki obligingly collapsed, ending the match after only twelve seconds. Gorgeous George's path to fame accelerated, his telegenic theatrics a perfect match for the burgeoning age of television. Siki would be dead within a year, a relative unknown today, yet far more deserving of recognition. Siki won numerous matches in this career, but due to the color of his skin his name was never entered in the record books.

Born Reginald Berry in Kansas City, Missouri, in 1899, Siki was—according to an article on the Slam Wrestling site—among the most prominent Black athletes of his day, achieving fame largely in Eastern Europe, where he could escape from the rampant racism of North America (in Canada the press once dubbed him "gorilla man"). After performing for a stretch in Germany in the months leading up to World War II, Siki and his wife were arrested in 1942 and imprisoned in Tittmoning, a medieval castle in Bavaria, along with hundreds of Americans. Siki nearly starved to death. At one point, a fellow inmate, Max Brandel, drew a caricature of him which Siki inscribed with the words, "Let's keep going."

I learned the story of Siki when I met up with his great-great-grandson, James Lott Jr., in Zoom-land recently to further my deep dive into the varied lives of grandpas. James, fifty-five, has a detonation of black hair that expands out in all directions, a neatly trimmed white goatee, and a vibrant and friendly personality. He has a whole string of letters after his name—CTACC, CDC, LVN, PMO, OA, DD—that speak to his thirst for learning. "I'm a chameleon of many sorts," James said. I'd call that an understatement. James is the CEO and founder of both JLJ Media and Super Organizer. He is certified as a professional organizer and life coach, holds a nursing degree and a PhD, has done acting gigs on commercials and an episode of *House* (season four, episode four), has his own YouTube channel, and does a podcast called *Really! I'm a Grandparent!* James, who's single, lives in Englewood, California, and stays close to his many nearby grandchildren.

James started his career as a farm and agricultural insurance specialist, but during the recession of 2008 he had a major epiphany. "I realized I hated my job," he told me, "hated everything in the city. My kids were grown, and I'd already become a grandfather. I decided to change my whole life." He made a list of all the things he loved to do. "I like filing. I like organizing. I like people.

I like media. I don't mind speaking in front of people. So, I talked about it with my grandfather's sister, and she said, 'There's a business in there. Entrepreneurship!'" James moved back to his family home in Los Angeles and started Super Organizer LLC, providing organizational services to a growing roster of clients that today includes movie stars. He also followed his passion for video and podcasting, with a flair for being on camera. The media world is James's version of the Forever Letter. "My grandkids know me as this person who talks to celebrities. When I die, they can just go online and see their grandfather."

When I learned that James became a grandpa at the tender young age of thirty-nine, I said, "Wow, I thought I was young at fifty-five when my first grandkid was born. You were way ahead of me!"

"Here's the deal," James replied. "I started my podcast because I saw the face of grandparenting has changed. My show is for young grandparents. I come from a long line of them. I grew up with grandparents who still jogged and dated and were having kids." When James told me this I tried, and failed, to imagine the grandparents in my life jogging. The only time I could imagine them moving that quickly was to run away from bears.

One of James's grandfathers—Grandpa Bob—was an executive with Chase Bank in Manhattan. "He was young, a rolling stone," James said. "Dressed very sharp, smoked a cigar, totally New York, the whole thing." James's other grandfather was white and Dutch, a little older, with a white beard. "My two grandfathers were like chess pieces on opposite sides of the board." One of James's youthful grandmothers would start her day running ten miles and swimming five. She drove a sporty Karmann Ghia.

Through his podcast, James has connected with all kinds of young grandparents. "I'm meeting more and more people in their thirties and forties who are grandparents," he said. "It's no

Photo courtesy of Bonita Lott

James Lott Jr. on granny's Karmann Ghia.

big deal in their lives. It's like, 'I had a daughter at eighteen, and she had a child at eighteen." Being a single grandpa who's active in the LA dating scene is also a different ball game. "I never know when to bring it up," James said. "Sometimes it comes out organically, like, 'What are you doing this weekend? I'm seeing my grandkids in Sacramento.' It's a mixed reaction."

James also sees that many of today's youthful grandfathers are playing a larger role in the lives of their grandkids. "I always think it's a generational thing. A lot of times the grandmother is seen as the nucleus of the family, but there are some good grandfathers out there who do run families. It's part of my mission to share that."

"The second thing for me," James continued, "is the multiracial aspect. I have grandkids that look the spectrum from blond hair and freckles to brown." During the period of civil unrest after the George Floyd killing, James had honest talks with his grandkids about the police based on his own negative experiences. The brown grandkids got a different talk than the blond ones. "But the Gen Zs and Gen Alphas," James said, "they're actually not caught up in all that suff. *We're* the ones caught up in it—we boomers and millennials. My grandkids have a set of friends whose parents were same sex. Their first president was Black. So their whole outlook is different."

James has found there's a generational shift in perspectives on work-life balance as well, with many young people choosing educational and career paths outside the norms pounded into us by our greatest generation parents. "These kids are saying, you want to pay me ten dollars an hour to do *that*?" James said. "They're questioning. Some are choosing trade schools instead of college. I was taught to work at a job until you're sixty-five and then you retire and travel. I'm actually impressed with how much these kids don't care about certain things that we're holding on to. They just want to live their lives. They're going to do it their way."

This idea resonated with me—a lot—when I thought about it within the context of nurturing the next great generation. Being fully accepting of differences and unconstrained by old-fashioned career paths seem all part of the same new vision. And these changes seem to be happening naturally as a result of the guidance and wisdom we gave our children when we were young parents. We—and I mean "we" in the larger sense meaning so many parents everywhere—taught our kids to treat everyone the same. We also encouraged them to choose the career that would allow them to do what they loved, even if that meant making less money. By the time our kids left the house as young adults, we'd largely completed our job. And through that parenting—ours and James's alike (and yours)—the newest generation is already greater in many ways than any that came before. James summed it up best when he said, "They have the freedom to live a different life."

This doesn't mean we grandparents can't continue to play a strong supportive role. We can help lead a discussion about generational greatness. And we will always be the elder maple trees whose leaves nurture the seedlings. We can, like Aunt Lois said, be there for them. But we have to be careful not to preach to them like we know everything, because we don't. Tom Brokaw said he learned more from his grandkids than they've learned from him. Wise words.

I saw this principle on glorious display on a warm July day a few years ago on the shores of Lake Willoughby, a place I will continue to return to in this book. All our grandkids and their cousins were down at the beach with their parents, and everyone was buzzing with excitement because we knew that this was the day that my cousin's son, William, would become engaged to his boyfriend, Brendon. The plan was that Brendon would take William out on their vintage wooden motorboat and pop the question. The grandkids made signs of congratulations that they could hold up when the boat returned to the shore, and sure enough, an hour later as the boat approached—William and Brendon beaming—the grandkids jumped up and down on the dock with their signs, shouting "Yay!" and "Congratulations!" and "We love you!" Nobody on the beach that day had to explain that William and Brendon were different, that they were gay. Because they are, in fact, no different than any of us. They are simply a young couple in love, one that is today happily married.

Before James and I parted ways in Zoom-land, I asked him for his number one piece of wisdom for the next generation. He instantly said, "You can survive anything. Life isn't fair. Life is tough. Life is wonderful. It's all those things, three dimensional. I wish I could have told myself that when I was eighteen. Just don't worry, James. You will go through a lot of stuff, but you will survive, and that's what I tell my grandkids."

Our ancestors continue to shape who we are now, through genetics and remembrance. When James talked about survival, all I could picture was the greatest wrestler of the twentieth century, the indomitable Reginald Siki, languishing in a German prison camp, so hungry he lay still to conserve energy, yet he smiled as he looked at the caricature drawn of him and wrote the words I will say to my loved ones any time our multidimensional lives get tough: "*Let's keep going.*"

CHAPTER 17

The Kim Long Orphanage

The kamikaze circled near the island of Okinawa, peering through the scattered clouds to spot enemy ships, while below him aboard a US Navy armed transport the young lieutenant who would become my father manned his radar station, on the lookout for another blip that could end his life. Perhaps at that instant they both spotted each other. Lieutenant Bill Page shouted the alert into his intercom with the location of the incoming kamikaze as the pilot sent his plane into a deep dive. Aboard the ship, panic ensued as it had repeatedly for over a week as wave after wave of kamikaze had attacked. The captain shouted orders, "Smoke! Smoke!" to shroud the ship from view, but it was too late; the pilot leveled off and headed straight at the ship at bow level. My father heard the ship's guns open up in a roar and saw the kamikaze getting closer and closer, seeming to grow in size, closer and closer, before the plane was finally blasted into disintegration, shards of steel splashing across the tops of the waves just feet from the side of the ship. My father stared in horror at the severed leg of the pilot floating in bloody water.

Dad aboard the USS Burleigh, back row, eleventh from left.

Like so many veterans, my father rarely talked about his war experiences. It was only when I was a teenager that I began to understand how deeply wounded he was emotionally. His PTSD would show itself unexpectedly and with terrifying effect. I once saw my mom hand him a bowl of cereal. He took one look at the bowl, which was red, and his entire face contorted into a fierce mask of terror with clenched teeth and fiery eyes as he screamed, "Blood!"

The trauma of war—which never fully left him—led my father to fight for world peace and show kindness to others throughout his long life. Years after he'd retired from Polaroid (and become a grandpa many times over) he was not content to lounge on a beach. He'd ensconce himself in his office overlooking the mountains and focus his prodigious mind on solving problems for humanity. One day he wrote a letter to a manager with the Vermont Department of Corrections named John Downs, asking, "How would you like to reduce rates of recidivism and improve lives through a better understanding of human nature?" Downs and a colleague, Rick Perry, took him up on the offer. Dad taught John and Rick about the teachings of Harvard professor E. O. Wilson on the epigenetic rules, a set of genetically driven human behaviors. The result was the nation's first implementation of what's become known as restorative justice. Instead of locking up people who'd committed crimes (where they'd learn to become better criminals while in jail), the state began mandating that offenders publicly apologize to their victims, acknowledge their guilt, then make amends. For example, instead of locking up two guys who'd burned down a covered bridge, the offenders apologized, learned carpentry, and rebuilt the bridge. They got jobs in construction and became productive members of society. Restorative justice has since been adopted by dozens of states and many countries around the world. My dad was a classic unsung hero.

The example set by him made me think more deeply about the importance of service, particularly the service of our veterans. How can serving others shine a light on better ways to nurture our grandchildren? Who are the unsung grandpa heroes of today who are making a difference?

I started my search for veteran wisdom by reaching out to my buddy Greg Payne, host of the *Cool Grandpa* podcast, to see who he could introduce me to. Greg has interviewed dozens of grandpas on his excellent show. Before long I was face-to-face in Zoom-land with Ralph Jodice, a retired three-star air force general from south central Pennsylvania. Ralph—nicknamed Dice by his fellow airmen—rose through the ranks flying an F-111 fighter-bomber, a jet that can travel faster than the speed of sound and carry nuclear payloads. In 2011, Ralph was the NATO air component commander for Operation Unified Protector in Libya, enforcing a no-fly zone to safeguard civilians. I figured a guy who could fly a supersonic fighter-bomber and run complex NATO operations would have a few things to say about being a good grandpa.

Ralph, sixty-nine, is fit and gregarious, with chiseled features and a down-to-earth, no-nonsense manner. He grew up in Bergen County, New Jersey, where his dad served as the chief of police. Ralph's maternal grandparents were of German/Danish stock, while his paternal grandparents immigrated to America from Naples and Sicily, Italy, greeted by the Statue of Liberty in 1904. Ralph and his wife, Judy, raised three sons, and today they have seven grandchildren, the oldest a teenager.

I asked Ralph how his experience serving in the military informed his life as a dad and grandpa. "I'm a firm believer in setting an example," Ralph said. "Besides doing various jobs with the air force, I made sure I was there for my sons. I coached their soccer and basketball teams when they were in grammar school. I made the time. My sons saw that—what it means to serve and volunteer—and our grandchildren have seen that from the time they can remember." Ralph's family also saw his dedication to helping others in the larger community. He and Judy got involved in supporting the Palmer Home for Children, a foster care facility run by a local Presbyterian church. During one Thanksgiving in the mid-1980s, they were asked by their church if they would host a young five-year-old named Scott, who appeared to be struggling. They decided to take him under their wings. "Scott's about as close to being a foster son without being a foster son as you can get," Ralph said. Scott, now forty-three, has three sons of his own.

Ralph retired from the air force in 2013 after thirty-six years of service and became busier than ever. He's a member of his local Rotary Club, where he's served as the president, and been very active with a global organization called F3, which stands for Fitness, Fellowship, and Faith (the last of which is defined as simply a belief in something bigger than yourself). The mission of F3 is to "plant, grow, and serve small workout groups for men for the invigoration of male community leadership." I checked out a few videos on the F3 website of the grueling workouts, which always take place outside, rain or shine, and just looking at them made me want to lay down and have a nap. As in the air force, F3 members have nicknames. F3's current CEO, Frank Schwartz, is known as Dark Helmet. Ralph does talks at civic events and schools, where he shares a PowerPoint detailing his Eight Core Attributes of Service. These are:

Dedication: To a set of ideals or to a purpose... a mission.

Commitment to excellence: It's not about being perfect. It's about doing your best and letting the rest take care of itself.

Discipline: To see any task through to completion.

Courage: To stand up for what is right and to give of yourself. Every vocation requires sacrifice.

Loyalty: To those you serve with, and to the organization you serve in.

Strength: Physical and character.

Fortitude: To endure hardships.

Compassion: For every fellow human being and sharing in their pain. Treating every member of your community as if they are a member of our family.

When not doing push-ups in the rain, Ralph joins Judy volunteering for Roots for Boots, a local grassroots veterans support organization. Every year, the Jodice family has a get-together they call Camp Nonna (Judy's grandma name is Nonna). "We have the grandkids here for five or six days," Ralph said, "and some of them have come with us to deliver food to veterans."

The more I learned about Ralph's life of service, the more I was reminded of the letter my dad wrote to his sons that was so full of hope for our country. Hope rooted in our responsibilities as active citizens. I mentioned this to Ralph to get his thoughts on how we could instill this sense of hope in today's grandchildren in our age of divisiveness. "I think letting them see that we're not getting caught in the quagmire," Ralph answered. "We can disagree, but don't get rude, crude, and socially unacceptable about it. Nobody yelling at each other—in the air force we called that 'high and right.' It's the worse place to be."

Ralph went on to tell me about a trip one of his sons took up the East Coast to visit the Statue of Liberty. "We try to do some things like that with our grandchildren, too," Ralph said, "and when we see something like that we go, 'Hey, there is greatness in the world.' And again, I think by trying to set that example of calling those things out and making them aware matters."

I asked Ralph for his number one top priority wisdom for the next generation. He replied, "I used to say this when I was a commander at different times—you're always going to need a key message that's short, direct, and that people can understand, right? For me, it's, 'Do the right thing. Do the right things right. And do the right things right for the right reasons.' That's the mantra, the platform, the bully pulpit for our grandchildren to set them up for success."

* * *

I HAPPENED UPON THE NEXT grandpa veteran in my learning journey by chance a few weeks ago at the annual Patriot's Day celebration in my hometown. I was babysitting my two grandgirls and decided to take them out to explore the various events taking place just down the road. It was perfect spring weather, sunny and warm, with daffodils and forsythia blooming bright yellow and the lawns newly green after their winter sleep. We stopped at the visitors' center for an event commemorating those who had served on the many US Navy ships named *Lexington* over the years. The Lexington High School band was playing Sousa marches, while dignitaries and veterans mingled with families, and ladies dressed in colonial dresses handed out programs for the day's events. The Buckman Tavern, where the Minutemen gathered before confronting the British at the first battle of the revolution, was nearby. In the midst of this bustling scene, Gresh Lattimore, a retired captain in the US Navy Reserve, rose to the podium in his blue uniform and white hat. I was able to hear him speak only briefly to the meaning of service and sacrifice before one of my grandgirls needed a potty break. (This, of course, is the nature of grandparenting in a nutshell: profundity and the potty share my mental space in equal measure.) But within a few days Gresh and I managed to meet up over coffee.

Gresh is a compact eighty-two-year-old who brims with warmth, his thinning strawberry-blond hair above a lined and ruddy face. Beside him on the table was his navy cap with the name of the ship he served on, the fabled USS *Coral Sea* aircraft carrier. I started by asking Gresh about his early years. "You know," Gresh said, "I grew up with great white privilege. We go into a restaurant like this, we expect to be treated with dignity and respect. We don't face slights in our lives. It's

Gresh Lattimore

something I'm grateful for, but I lament that so many people haven't had the good experience growing up that I had." Gresh's dad was an engineer for Westinghouse while his mom stayed home to care for the family. He graduated from the University of the South in Sewanee, Tennessee, earning a scholarship to the Fletcher School at Tufts upon graduation. It was at Tufts where Gresh met his wife, Nancy, the love of his life. Tufts was also where Gresh first came in contact with midcareer naval officers. "They'd done something I hadn't," Gresh said. "They'd left the desk and gone to sea, been in the real world, had some adventure." With the Vietnam War underway, Gresh decided then and there to attend Officer Candidate School in Newport, Rhode Island. "I became a four-month wonder and was assigned to my ship. That was in 1966."

Thus began a life of service that extended far beyond his three-year stint as an ensign aboard his carrier off Vietnam's Gulf of Tonkin. In his second year of duty he served on the flight deck as an air transfer officer, coordinating logistics for takeoffs and landings. After returning home, Gresh earned a PhD in German affairs at the Fletcher School and ultimately went into small business lending at banks in the greater Boston area, a career spanning thirty years. But he always maintained his close ties with the US Navy, joining the navy reserves where he served until retiring in 1990. "I just loved that duty," Gresh said, "because I love being around military people."

Even when he technically retired from the navy, Gresh continued serving by volunteering to help veterans at the VA. He became a facilitator in a support group for Vietnam combat veterans suffering from PTSD. "I was there to listen, just listen," Gresh told me. "You got to know the guys and they got to know you. I really enjoyed that because I thought I was giving back to my fellow military men, guys that had a very different military experience than I had." (Another volunteer, who worked alongside Gresh at the VA, was a first responder at Ground Zero on 9/11.)

Gresh's service to his fellow veterans continued when he entered a new chapter of his life. "I became interested in hospice when I left banking. I wanted to give back to the community and have religion play a more important role in my life." Gresh took a three-year course in hospice training at St. Elizabeth's Medical Center, after which he became a regular visitor at the new hospice-care facility at his local VA. "They all had terminal diagnoses," he said. "I often brought my golden retriever with me." As Gresh talked about his hospice experience, what he termed "the ministry of presence," I was reminded of what my aunt Lois had told me: *Be there for them*. I realized something that should have been obvious all along, that being there matters for everyone, not just for our grandkids. Picturing Gresh and his dog bedside with a veteran in those final moments of life was so touching I forgot for a moment where I was, but my mind returned in time to hear the rest of Gresh's story.

After having heart surgery in 2019, Gresh had to scale back his volunteering at the VA, but he has continued to stay close to the veteran community. He's served for many years as the chairman of the ROTC program at Tufts University. He also volunteers at his Episcopal church. "I want to do whatever I can," Gresh said. "A motto of one of my support groups is, 'We never stop serving.' There's so much more out there beyond ourselves."

I asked Gresh about his experiences as a dad and today as a grandpa. "I have one son, Mark," Gresh told me. "He was adopted. We had some fertility issues. My sister had married a Colombian national and was a doctor, so she went to an orphanage in Medellín in 1975 and found our new son." Gresh had to fight back tears when he continued, "I can remember getting off the plane and my sister walked up with this little baby and hands him to me—'Here's your son.'" Today, Mark and his wife have two sons of their own. "We were delighted," Gresh said. "We raised him to become a man, and now he's raising his two kids. We made it clear to Mark that we wanted to be part of our grandkids' lives moving forward." Gresh and his wife visit their grandsons in New Jersey on a regular basis and have additional face time with them on Zoom.

I asked Gresh for the number one thing that mattered. He smiled and replied, "I would say first, find a good woman as a companion on your journey through life. You're sharing everything. Second, join the military. Wherever I go, if there's a fellow military person, I would be instantly open to helping him or her do anything."

* * *

I LEARNED ABOUT THE NEXT veteran I met thanks to a gentleman who reached out to me through my blog—the subject line, "Have you heard the story of Bob Staranowicz?" As I go through my journey of discovery, I never know what doors will open next. I often feel like I'm not writing the book, the book is writing me. I had a gut sense this email was something I needed to follow up on, and I'm glad I did. When Bob told me his story, it unspooled like a movie in my mind, a Francis Ford Coppola movie no less.

Bob was born in 1948 in the poor Fishtown neighborhood of Philadelphia, the son of a tailor. "I grew up in a house with a coal stove where the heat never reached the second floor," Bob told me. "There was one time my older brother was on the third floor, and when he woke up in the morning the glass of water by his bed was ice." When the Vietnam War was raging, Bob saw a lot of his friends getting drafted and being shipped off to war zones. Bob decided to have more control of his fate. "So, I joined up in '68," Bob said, "which let me pick my own school—a thirty-eight-week army electronics course at Fort Monmouth in New Jersey. But I ended up with the 101st Airborne, which was a shock." Most of Bob's friends in Vietnam were in the relatively safe Saigon area, while Bob found himself thirty minutes from the DMZ living in a hooch (a sandbag-covered hut that housed eight men) and getting shelled on a regular basis. "We had no running water and our showers were always cold," Bob said.

Bob put his army training to work within the communications security department, working in a repair shop and delivering equipment to firebases and outposts "in the middle of nowhere."

In April of 1970, a pitched battle was underway at Firebase Ripcord, a hilltop base manned by the 101st Airborne Division. Pitted against them on all sides were reinforced divisions of the Viet Cong. So many US soldiers were being killed an urgent call went out for reinforcements. "There were these two guys in my unit that were picked out to go to Ripcord," Bob said. "But they went out on sick call. I see them coming back, saying, 'We got out of it.'" Two of Bob's friends got picked instead. Both died in action. "They weren't even supposed to be there," he said. "I get choked up just talking about it."

Bob's pain, sadness, and relentless fear in the remote outpost amounted to a hell on earth, but fate soon brought him in contact with a better place, one that would change the trajectory of his life and the lives of others. "Sunday mornings, we used to send out our laundry, and it would come back all clean and I never knew where it went," Bob said. "So our company clerk was looking for somebody to go out with him to help deliver the laundry to where it was being cleaned, and I went with him." They drove across a wooden bridge over the Perfume River by the ancient imperial citadel of the city of Hue and soon arrived at the Kim Long Orphanage. Run by Catholic nuns, the orphanage cared for about one hundred children who'd lost their parents or been abandoned by their families due to disabilities.

"All of a sudden these kids start running at us," Bob said, "and it was just such an experience it's stayed with me to this day." Bob played with the kids, finding a brief, peaceful respite from the grinding worries of war. Not long after this he managed to land the plum job of mail clerk. This meant he had his own jeep to deliver the mail—and to visit the orphanage more often. Family and friends back in Philly sent him toys and candy to give the kids. "We weren't there for war," Bob said. "We were there for humanitarian reasons. If the stuff we did was reported on the news, we probably would have had different greetings when we got home."

Bob returned to Philly after his year of duty, walking proudly through the airport in his uniform pinned with the many medals he'd earned. A woman spat on him. Later, he had an encounter that was even worse. "I went to my old neighborhood and one of my best friends came up to me and said, 'Welcome home, baby killer.' He walked away, and I haven't seen or talked to him since. I heard that he went to Canada to avoid the draft."

Bob did his best to put the war behind him. He got married shortly after coming home, raised two daughters, and had a successful career in data management for companies including AT&T and IBM. He never talked about his war experiences with his family, basically doing everything he could to forget about it. That changed in 1992 when a nephew pressed him with questions about what he remembered about Vietnam. Bob opened up for the first time since coming home, and what his nephew heard blew him away. Bob embarked on writing a book about his experiences, titled *Chapter One*. Memories of Kim Long flooded back to him—holding the babies in his arms as they slept, playing with the children, the kind nuns who welcomed him in, the small white church. Compelled by the need to give back, Bob organized a fund drive to support the ongoing work of the orphanage. Each year since, with the generous contributions of family and friends, the orphanage has received thousands of dollars to pay for things like washing machines or health care for the children. In January of 2009, Bob and his youngest daughter returned to the orphanage to visit and spend time with a new generation of children (and hand-deliver another check). The church at the orphanage had been renamed Bob's Church.

All of this, however, was simply a prelude to the part of Bob's story I found most remarkable. Forty-seven years after leaving Vietnam, a woman who'd read about him and the orphanage reached out to ask if he was in fact one of the veterans who cared for the children at Kim Long—*because she was one of those children*. It turned out another US soldier, Lieutenant Frank Congiusta, also visited the orphanage the same year as Bob, and on one of those visits a fourteen-month-old baby girl named Le Thi Hung reached up her arms to him. With his wife's blessing, Frank brought Li home and adopted her. Her name became Laura, and she grew up in Frank's loving Italian family in Brooklyn. "I think she chose me more than I chose her!" Frank later told reporters. Frank and Laura came to Bob's house for an emotional reunion.

Today, Bob and his wife are blessed with three grandchildren, including a granddaughter he's especially close to because she lives nearby. When I asked Bob for the number one thing, he looked thoughtful for a long while. Then he said, "Since my granddaughter, Avery, was a little girl she's been going to the Memorial Day parade with me, which I've marched in. She's been to every parade I've been in, and I think she understands when she sees the groups I belong to—the VFW, the American Legion, Vietnam Veterans of America, Disabled American Veterans—how much we should be honoring veterans. That's the one thing I'd like her to remember." Each year in May, Avery helps Bob replace old flags on veterans' graves.

It took me a few days to process everything I'd heard from Ralph, Gresh, and Bob. All the conversations moved me deeply, but it wasn't until I stepped back and thought about them in unison that the real impact set in. I was amazed that all three men shared life stories that involved orphans or children in foster care. To be clear, I didn't know anything about these men prior to talking with them, other than that they were veterans who had served in different branches of the miliary. Yet they each experienced a call of duty that didn't involve firing a gun—it was the exact opposite. They were fathers first and foremost, men who responded when a child raised up their arms to them.

Another main takeaway was that their service never ended, and never will. They're each following their own unique interests yet all focused on helping others outside their immediate families. This speaks volumes about the collective impact of veterans. I can only wonder how many people have been uplifted by them, how many people in hospice in their last days were comforted by veterans like Gresh, how many children in foster care have found loving mentors like Ralph and his wife, or have run—joyously—out the door of an orphanage to play with soldiers like Bob.

My ultimate takeaway, however, is a bigger idea. I set out with the goal of collecting wisdom that could be instilled in our grandchildren. It was about changing *them* and *their* futures. But what I've come to realize is that I'm the one who needs to change. Gresh, Ralph, and Bob lead by example. Their life's work shines a light on a path that the youngest children can follow, whether that's supporting an orphanage, being there for those in hospice, delivering food to veterans in need, or a million other things. And what have I done? Practically nothing. I'll be turning sixty-six this year, and it's too late to turn back the clock. All I have is today and the future to set an example for my grandchildren. I'm determined to rethink my age not as an accumulation of years but as simple addition: 6 + 6 = 12. If I were twelve years old and my whole life was ahead of me, what would I do to help others? It's time for me to give back.

I'm starting with the place that's meant so much to Bob Staranowicz. My publisher, Regalo Press, has a philanthropic business model. Upon publication of one of their titles, they make a donation to a nonprofit chosen by the author. Mine will be the Kim Long Orphanage in Hue, Vietnam. For me, that orphanage is more than one place. It's symbolic of peace. When we reach out to help children, or when we sit quietly at someone's bedside in their last minutes, we bring peace to them and to ourselves. That's what my dad wanted and needed desperately, the balm for his kamikaze wounds. So, Dad, this one's for you.

CHAPTER 18

Let There Be Light

At 4:00 A.M. on April 8, 2024, the alarm went off. My wife and I groggily pulled ourselves from under the warm covers, drank copious amounts of strong coffee, and hit the road to make the journey up to northern Vermont to see the eclipse. Initially, we hadn't planned on going anywhere that day; we'd reasoned that we could see a pretty good eclipse from our home outside Boston without dealing with traffic and the expected hordes in the north country. But as the frenzy around "the Totality" grew we didn't want to miss out on the main event, and if that meant being sleep deprived, so be it. When we arrived at our home in Vermont, the place was a honeycomb abuzz with friends and family, including our grandsons, Henry and Charlie. It was a brilliantly sunny day, the sky a cool blue expanse—a remarkable stroke of luck in a mountainous corner of the state that often resembles a rainforest.

The excitement grew as the day progressed. Viewing glasses at the ready; snacks prepared; an extra sweater packed in anticipation of the drop in temperature when the sun hid. By early afternoon, we'd all gathered down at the beach on Lake Willoughby, everyone chatting, the children darting around us like atoms, the whole scene humming to a growing pitch as the time of the eclipse approached. I sat in a lawn chair next to my grandsons. At precisely 2:16:35 P.M., the slightest indent could be observed on one side of the sun, a sliver of darkness.

"I see it!" Henry shouted. "Me too!" said Charlie. A dozen adults intoned "ooooh" and "aaaaah," a chorus of rising astonishment as the sliver grew and grew, minute by minute. I looked through my tinted visor for a long while, but at a certain point—close to the moment of the Totality at 3:29—I found the more

My grandsons, Henry and Charlie, seeing the eclipse.

fascinating spectacle to be the tonality of the light all around us on the beach and the rippling waters and the green mountains rising on the opposite shore. I'd never seen anything like it. The light combined aspects of dusk yet with a higher contrast and crispness, growing darker with each second as the moon moved across the sun, and yet somehow the light retained itself, as if darkness and light had for this brief time found a way to coexist, and then a countdown began, a chorus of...

"Ten!"

"Nine!"

"Eight!"

"Seven!"

"Six!"

"Five!"

"Four!"

"Three!"

"Two!"

"One!"

I stared up at the sight of the full black moon surrounded by a shimmering circular yellow flare of luminescence radiating out into the dimly dark blue sky, and in plainly physical terms what I did next was stand up, but it felt more as if I was ejected up—or perhaps pulled—to my feet, and when I looked around at everyone on the beach I could see the round "O" of the Totality reflected in the shape of mouths dropped in wonder. I snapped a picture of my grandsons as they stared, transfixed, then I turned my gaze back to the sky. Insofar as someone can think at all in a moment like that, the thought that arose in my mind was that this extraordinary vision explained where religion came from. The eclipse was so stunningly beautiful it spoke eloquently of a higher power.

The Totality, Lake Willoughby, Vermont.

My heavenly eclipse experience helped me see a recurring theme emerging in my many conversations with grandfathers. Again and again, one word kept coming up. The word was God.

Eric Behr found his path back to God through the power of prayer to heal his granddaughter. Bob Halperin's Forever Letters are rooted in ancient Jewish traditions and the Old Testament. Saif Shahpurwala's Muslim faith guides his daily prayer rituals and sense of gratitude. Several of the veterans I met with serve others through their church groups. This undercurrent of spirituality within the grandpa community made me want to explore the role of religion in shaping the next great generation.

I'll have to admit at the outset that organized religion has not been a big part of my own life. When I was growing up, we said the Lord's Prayer at holiday dinners, we went to church on Sundays and sang hymns. But there was no cross behind the pulpit. As Unitarians we sought to find commonalities among all religions and select the tastiest philosophies to put on our cafeteria trays. When our kids were little, we brought them to church but never pushed them to take religious education classes.

When they got older, I came to realize how little of the traditional things they had learned. My son saw the album cover for the soundtrack to *The Mission,* starring Robert De Niro, showing a man on a cross floating on the Amazon toward a waterfall, and he made the reasonable assumption that this was how Jesus died. It wasn't just being nailed to the cross that did him in, it was the cross/waterfall combo. This was kind of funny and horrifying at the same time. We had failed so miserably in the religious education department. And yet we did manage to drive home the importance of the Golden Rule, and our kids grew up to be very fine adults. Nevertheless, I've always sensed there's a trove of religious knowledge that I've never tapped into. So, I asked myself, What would the leaders of the world's major religions have to say about their role as grandfathers? What wisdom could they impart that's informed by their faith?

I started down this path—the red carpet of life's sanctuary—by meeting Father Craig Burlington, a retired Episcopalian priest. Craig, eighty, is gregarious and warm, with a long face and a dulcet baritone voice that welcomed me in. Our conversation was one-on-one in Zoom-land, yet I felt like I was in his church for the first time as he began to tell me his story.

Craig was born in a small town in New Jersey, the son of parents in crisis. "My father had a mental illness," Craig said. "He was bipolar. A psychiatrist told my mother, 'If you want to bring up your child with some sense of normalcy, you're not going to get it in this situation.'" Craig's mother's father, the grandpa he came to know as Pop-Pop, took them away to Florida and arranged for a divorce. Craig grew up without a father. After college, he joined the ministry, got married, and settled down to raise four children. "I had a real lack of sense of who my father was," Craig said, "and became the dad I didn't have." That changed later in his life when—at the urging of his mother—he sought out his father and finally got to know him. Thanks to medication, his father's life had stabilized to some degree and he'd remarried.

Craig and his dad had a wonderful relationship spanning fifteen years, and thankfully his dad was able to get to know Craig's kids as well. "We have a wonderful picture taken on Father's Day of my dad and me and our four kids, which turned out unfortunately to be his last picture." His dad died in 1979 at the age of sixty-three, in a psychiatric hospital.

I asked Craig what he remembered most about his grandfather. "Oh, my Pop-Pop was a wonderful, wonderful man that I knew only until I was six years old. Pop-Pop was a sweetheart and he loved cars. He would take me out on Sunday rides in his 1938 Hudson." Craig's memory of Pop-Pop's passing is vivid to this day. "We went to the graveside," Craig said, "and it was covered in flowers. It was beautiful. We said the Lord's Prayer there and were very, very sad. I went to the grave a couple of weeks later, and lo and behold in my little six-year-old mind, I thought they had taken him away because all the flowers were gone and it was just a flat grassy surface. And I was told, 'No, Grampy's down under the ground.' And I went to that grave for the rest of my life and even took my first child there." Throughout Craig's childhood his grandmother would talk with him about his grandfather and how much he meant to him. "She said, 'He loved you so much, Craig, he worshipped the ground you walked on.' And I remember taking that to heart; it was like a prototype of God's love for us. I preach about this all the time, that you are so loved by an eternal force in your life which is right inside your heart."

Craig's words led me to delve deeper into childhood experiences that may have drawn him to the priesthood. "As a little boy, my mother always made sure we went to church," Craig said. "I can remember being in the pew in St. John's Church a great deal, kneeling and praying for God to take care of my mother. I had a sense of God's presence. I remember watching our priest,

Mr. Whitmarsh, in his vestments walking in the procession, the choir singing, the crucifers carrying the cross, the candle bearers, and I felt hugely at home. It was enough to anchor me in a God awareness that was so deep it took root, and it was very influential in discerning my vocation."

Craig found his ministry to be hugely fulfilling. He was always present for others at their times of greatest joy and need, serving most recently as rector at St. Luke's in East Greenwich, Rhode Island, before retiring at the age of sixty-six and moving to Florida. Craig was speaking to me while on his third-floor balcony there, looking out at the water and greenery below. "There's a fountain right in front of me," Craig said, "and it's flowing up in a huge white stream with two side streams, so for me that's an icon of God the Father, God the Son, and God the Holy Spirit. It's a three-part fountain. I sit here every morning and do my morning prayer."

Today, Craig and his wife have eight grandchildren—four boys and four girls. "Those children are the joy in my life," he told me. Retirement from the priesthood hasn't dimmed his passion for teaching and mentoring the young people lucky enough to be in his flock. "One of our retirement goals was to take each of our grandchildren when they were thirteen on some special trip to expose them to some good stuff," Craig said, "but also to have a very private time with them ourselves." One trip in particular stood out in Craig's mind, the year they took their granddaughters, Esther and Rebecca, to Normandy, France, to see the D-Day beaches where the tide of World War II had turned. His granddaughters had been studying the war in eighth grade and wanted to experience the battlefield firsthand. "We were in the huge cemetery with all the white crosses and at eleven o'clock they held a service in a courtyard," Craig said. "We had an unbelievable sense of identification with the grief of the horrible war and yet also honoring all those veterans who were buried there, and that really bonded us all together in a wonderful way."

I asked Craig the same question I'd asked Tom Brokaw, whose own visit to Normandy had been so transformative. Did our grandchildren have to experience a similarly existential crisis to forge them into the new greatest generation? Craig's brow furrowed as his answer rushed out. "The answer is definitely yes, of course. But what's so frightening about that question is that between the pandemic and the horror that we are going through right now in our very own country, not to mention Gaza and Israel and Ukraine, not to mention all the horrors around the world that are so apparent to our grandchildren's lives because of the media—it worries me because it is so much to take in. We read about it now all the time, how this generation is suffering from anxiety and from the divisiveness, and right this very weekend, all these protests in universities that hark back to the Vietnam War." Craig shared with me that one of his grandchildren is on medication for anxiety. "It hurts me," Craig said. "It hurts me."

I replied, "Craig, you're a retired priest, but you'll always be a priest, yes? You'll never stop being that person. If you could speak to these kids, what would you say to them?"

Craig's mood instantly changed, as if the Florida sun had come out from a cloud. "I do it! I do it!" he said excitedly. "I did the most wonderful series with these teenagers recently when a teacher asked me to come in and speak with these kids about peace and do the laying on of hands and anointing with oil. We had a meditation, then I said, 'Once you think about what I'm going to read, afterwards tell me what it means to you.' And these are the words they came up with: Calm. Silence. Jesus. Love. Harmony. Thanksgiving. Kindness. Forgiveness. Friendship. Grace. We have so much to give to our kids by helping them come up with those qualities themselves. I am convinced—because it's happened over and over again—that hope will be born anew. That's our entire Christian, Muslim, Jewish heritage. How we see that hope expressed varies according to our traditions. To us, it's the resurrection."

I asked Craig to think about everything he'd ever preached, everything he's ever wanted his children and grandchildren to know, and distill it into the holy water of one singular idea, the number one thing. "Love conquers all," Craig said with conviction. "Love your neighbor as yourself. Love and recognize that you are loved. And that love is the saving grace that we have as human beings, whether it's loving the creation, loving our pets, loving each other, loving our grandchildren, loving our grandparents, loving the memories we have even when you have been in mental illness. When you have been through divorce. When you have been through painful moments. It takes a while to go beneath the platitudes to the depths of what love means; it's the fire in your heart. God is love. As simple as that!"

As Craig was telling me this, I envisioned the end of the movie *Love Actually* in my mind, with loved ones embracing in the airport as the Beach Boys sing "God Only Knows." I've seen the movie about a dozen times and somehow it never gets old, and the reason why it stays fresh—and always makes me tear up—is because it's based on a foundational truth. Love is actually all around.

It was no coincidence that Craig referenced Muslim and Jewish heritage as part of an inclusive perspective on faith. Most religious leaders see the interconnected nature of religious belief and have the utmost respect for their peers. In fact, they often attend the same interdenominational conferences. Craig graciously opened up his network to me, and before long I was introduced to Dr. Abdul Hamid Samra, a Muslim imam currently living in Miami, Florida. I met up with Abdul Hamid in Zoom-land for a wonderful conversation where he shared his life story and wisdom for the next generation.

Abdul Hamid, seventy-two, has a round face with white hair and neatly trimmed white beard, and like Craig Burlington he spoke with the assurance of a man accustomed to addressing a congregation. Abdul Hamid was born in Damascus, Syria, the son of a farmer, and had seven brothers and sisters in a bustling household. One of his fondest childhood memories was being with his grandfather, Kamel. "My grandfather had a very big house with many rooms, and trees in a courtyard," Abdul Hamid said. "All the children and grandchildren lived in the same house. The grandfather and of course the grandmother, they are very respected, and everyone tried to compete to do good things to serve them." After the monthlong fast of Ramadan each year, the family held a joyful three-day celebration. "Grandfather would be there to give us money and candy, so we'd always look forward to that." When Abdul Hamid told me that his grandfather gave him candy, I instantly related because I often give my grandchildren chocolate for breakfast—not a lot, just a treat, but enough to show that life is sweet.

Abdul Hamid's relationship with his grandpa was sweet in many ways. "He was so soft and everything," Abdul Hamid said. "If I do anything my parents are not happy with, then I have the protection there. He would, you know, cover me for anything, but in a positive way. He wanted to teach me something good but at the same time show that he really loves me and does not like anything bad to happen to me."

When Abdul Hamid was fourteen, he experienced a transformation that would set the course for his life. Under the guidance of a ninety-five-year-old imam, Adul Hamid memorized the entire Quran by heart, six hundred pages comprised of six thousand two hundred and thirty-six verses. Abdul Hamid was just getting started. Once he'd learned the Quran, he was taught the exact way to recite and pronounce each and every verse. Only when he'd passed this test did his teacher give him a signed certification that would allow him to be an imam. Abdul Hamid explained that this tradition had been going on for centuries. "My teacher showed me his certification and said to me, 'I got this authority from my teachers, who got it from their teachers—teacher to teacher to teacher—all the way to Prophet Muhammed, and then from the Angel Gabriel, and then from God.'" Abdul Hamid was in fact the thirty-first generation in the chain of learning, originating over fifteen hundred years ago. I was struck by the similarities between the intergenerational transfer of learning among religious leaders and the wisdom passed down by grandparents. In some ways, we are all cut from the same cloth, even if we're not wearing vestments.

Abdul Hamid grew into the role of imam at the same time he pursued his education and career. He earned his bachelor's in electrical engineering in Syria before moving to the US in 1986, where he earned his master's and PhD. He taught at Florida International University (FIU) for many years and currently teaches at the University of Miami, all the while serving as an imam for the Islamic Center of Greater Miami. "I feel people are coming to me and they need help," Abdul Hamid said. "I have an obligation towards my community. My teachers, they spent time with me, so I owe that to the other generation."

Abdul Hamid married in 1983, and he and his wife raised four children, two boys and two girls. His family has been fruitful and multiplied. Today, he has five grandchildren. "When I'm with them I forget everything," Abdul Hamid said. "I just want to spend time with them. Play with them. Do I say I love them more than my own children? I would say yes! As a parent you're so busy with life and other things. Of course I love my children, but with the grandchildren I don't have the full responsibility, so I have more time to think and be more relaxed." Abdul Hamid also follows in his grandfather's footsteps, continuing post-Ramadan celebrations with the whole family. "I give my grandchildren money and special chocolate, but also I try to connect them to God by teaching them little verses of the Quran to memorize, and I explain what it means to pray, right? And above all emphasize being kind, being respectful, good morals, being honest. This is what makes them better people—implanting the idea of sacrifice and to share what God, what Allah, has given them."

It occurred to me that Adul Hamid was the second religious leader I'd spoken with who was living in Florida, a place the cable news shows call a "red state." And I'm in New England, a region some would call "solidly blue." So I asked him, "When did America become color coded? How can we help our grandchildren get past all this division?"

Abdul Hamid sighed. "You know," he said, "it is a fact that we are different. But again, if I go back to the Quran, it comes down to respecting one another, honoring each other, that should be always there. You may not agree with people, which is fine, but you still have respect for the people. We are as God told us, we are all the children of Adam. We came from the same father, same mother. We are human. This should be implanted in the next generation."

Abdul Hamid's use of the words "next generation" brought me back to the concept of making our grandchildren the greatest, and what it would take for that to come about.

Abdul Hamid replied, "The way I look at it is this: There are three parts of our self as a person. One is the body. One is intelligence of the mind. One is the soul. And we need to have a balance to nourish them. The nourishment for the body is to eat healthy and to exercise, and the nourishment for the mind is to keep on getting knowledge. Don't stop. And then we need the nourishment for the soul. And the nourishment for the soul is by helping other people—a charity or volunteering. If we can have that balance, then hopefully our next generation will be better than us."

From his earliest days in Damascus memorizing the Quran, to his many years of teaching, to leading prayers in the Muslim community, to his years of fatherhood and now grandfatherhood, I wanted to know what stood out as his singular number one thing that mattered the most.

"I would say, it's not worth it to have any conflict with another person. You can live a good life. God has blessed you with so many things. Think of the reward of God so you can be more easygoing and be able to forgive people, to get the peace of God inside you."

There were many ideas that Abdul Hamid shared with me that resonated, but one subtle thing jumped out. As a writer, I pay a lot of attention to words. The words we use to describe things matter a great deal because they often reveal our inner core. When Abdul Hamid spoke of ways to instill wisdom in grandchildren, the word he used most frequently was "implant." This was not a coincidence given that his father was a farmer. Abdul Hamid's family thrived thanks to their ability to grow healthy crops. This is a very apt metaphor for what we do as parents and grandparents. We do everything we can to ensure the next crop will be healthy and thrive.

Next up on my path toward understanding was a conversation with a rabbi, in this case Orthodox. I didn't have to go far. A fifteen-minute drive from home I found Beth Menachem Chabad of Newton, Massachusetts, and their most senior rabbi,

Chaim Prus. He greeted me at the door dressed in traditional Lubavitch garb, a black suit with white shirt. His friendly smile was framed by an ample white beard, and he had a twinkle in his eyes.

Chaim's story unfolded as we sat in a conference room of the Chabad center he founded. Chaim, seventy-three, was born in Tashkent, then part of the USSR, the son of a clothing manufacturer who struggled to make a living under the strictures of communist rule. He never knew any of his grandparents. "It was a time of war," Chaim said. "If you knew your parents, you were lucky." The fact that his parents survived was due to sheer tenacity. "My parents ran away," he said. "If they had stayed in the place where they were born, they would have been killed by the Nazis." Living in the USSR was no picnic for Orthodox Jews, to put it mildly. "They closed all the synagogues. The worst sin was to give Jewish education to children. If you were caught, you would get ten to twenty years in gulags."

Chaim's road to America was winding, starting with the family migrating to Latvia, then to Poland, then in 1960 settling in Israel. In 1967, as a teenager, Chaim was restless. Raised Orthodox, he found himself questioning everything (as teens do) and seeking affirmation of his religious path. He'd heard about the Orthodox Chabad movement centered in New York and wanted to learn more. "I don't accept authority," Chaim said. "I want to go see it myself. Is it really as meaningful and spiritual as they say? There's a lot of things in this world." His quest for understanding led him to the center of Lubavitch Judaism in the enclave of Crown Heights, Brooklyn, a vibrant Orthodox community led by the legendary Rabbi Menachem Mendel Schneerson. "There was a genius," Chaim said, holding up one finger. "He had a kind of inner divine inspiration. His look was permeating for me."

Rabbi Schneerson inspired thousands of young people—including Chaim—to join and spread the Lubavitcher movement to help guarantee the continuity of the Jewish people. "Instead of going into business, you'd start these Chabad institutions to reach out to young Jews and get them involved back in Judaism. It was volunteering."

Not only did Chaim find his true calling in Brooklyn, he also found the woman he would marry and have five children with—and nearly *forty* grandchildren. (When I heard of Chaim's experience in Crown Heights, I felt an immediate kinship—me, a WASP Unitarian, and an Orthodox rabbi. Go figure. I, too, lived in Crown Heights when I was a young man, and met my future wife there.)

With the blessing of Rabbi Schneerson, Chaim traveled to Boston and ultimately founded a whole new Chabad community.

I asked about Chaim's life today as a grandfather. He said, "When the kids are younger, there's a very strong connection with the grandparents because you kind of baby them, you're nice to them. You don't put restrictions like the parents, so you can give them candies and butter cookies. You know the old joke—Why do grandchildren and grandparents get along so well? They have a common enemy! But when they become teenagers, they become involved in their own life, right? What do I need to do, the old man?" Chaim answered his own question: "On a Shabbat or a special holiday, they want to come join together with the grandparents, be a part of them, especially if the grandparents are well educated in Jewish things. They can discuss it, they want your approval, your encouragement. We have the same values and goals in life. We want to make the world a better place through the divine teachings of the Torah. The younger generation has a different style, but the mission is the same, so we have much in common."

Importantly, Chaim talked at length about how he raised his children and how he interacts with them today, all with mutual respect and infused with the teachings of the Torah. His many grandchildren see these interactions and learn from them. "The kids absorb it, like a natural thing," Chaim said. "You learn how to ride a bike no matter how you get the bike, right? It becomes a part of you."

I wondered aloud if true generational greatness could be inculcated in this way, naturally in the peace of our homes, or if a crisis was required to forge children into greatness. "Well, let me give you a very simple example," Chaim said. "Firemen sit in the firehouse and play cards all day. This until when? Until the alarm rings and then they jump and risk their lives for others. What I'm trying to say is the following: World War II generation, the alarm bell rang and they responded. Our generation didn't have to go to Normandy beaches because the alarm didn't ring, right? The question is, What are your values? If we are able to instill the values of what is right and what is wrong—and I don't mean just Jewish, any belief—that there is a higher being, a higher judgment, if that is instilled in young people we can be pretty sure that when the alarm rings they will stand up the same as the generation before."

Whether those values are actually being instilled (or implanted) in the next generation is another matter altogether, one that Chaim felt was a big challenge for today's parents and grandparents. "Unfortunately, we have a situation where people are confused," he said. "They have no idea what is right or wrong. And I don't blame them because it was taken out of the educational systems. And I'm not here to say that my religion or your religion is better, no, I'm talking the concept that there is something higher, a judgment for whatever they do, the right and wrong. There is a fundamental concept of humanity. There is something greater than us."

I asked Chaim about the terrible divisions in our country, and in light of this what his number one essential advice would be. "If you share the same values in life, you already have something very much in common," Chaim said. "It can be Republican or Democrat, I'm not talking particulars. The real binding between generations is having the same core values, and that flows through everything else. That's how you will be ready when the bell rings."

Within a few days of my meeting with Chaim—with thoughts of the firemen jumping into action at the sound of the bell still reverberating in my mind—I met in Zoom-land with a Reform rabbi, Eric Gurvis, to gain another perspective. Eric, sixty-eight, has salt-and-pepper hair and a closely cropped beard. Right away he reminded me of the friends I grew up with in my Judeo-Christian hometown, talkative and full of energy. Eric was born in the Bronx about half a block from Yankee Stadium, the son of an accountant who worked for IBM. When Eric was six months old his family moved to Long Island, near Levittown. "It was a good suburban life," he said. "A lot of kids in the neighborhood playing in the street." When Eric was in the second grade, his parents realized their three sons needed some religious education, so they joined a synagogue around the corner, a place that Eric would ultimately come to see as an extension of the family's home. "We went to Shabbat every Friday night in my youth, the collation after the services, then went out for ice cream—the whole thing," Eric said. Getting together as a family, however, was not reserved only for Shabbat. They ate dinner together every night.

Eric knew all four of his grandparents, which is extremely rare in our age group. His grandparents, his parents, cousins, aunts, uncles, and brothers would hold yearly get-togethers in Florida, an opportunity for all the generations to bond. "I have a vivid memory of my oldest son, Benjamin, sitting on the couch with me and his grandfather, and my uncle David looking at us and saying, 'Holy cow, there are ninety years between them.' My grandfather was beaming."

As with all faith leaders, there was a turning point in Eric's life where his religion became something more, an irresistible call to a higher purpose. "The reality that synagogue was an extended family and community was so important," he said. "My involvement in youth group, helping to lead the worship with my childhood rabbi, somewhere in the midst of it all it kind of coalesced." In the tenth grade, Eric gave a speech at his confirmation service, starting out with Robert Frost's "The Road Not Taken." "It was a very profound piece of poetry for me," he said. "Upon reflection, I was signaling that I was going to go on a different path into the world working with the Jewish community." Eric went to rabbinical school, was ordained in 1983, and has since led congregations, including one in Jackson, Mississippi. "I always wanted to re-create what I had as a child," Eric said. "A synagogue community that felt like home. Where the people you met in the lobby or in the parking lot or the sanctuary were your family, and you felt safe."

Becoming a grandfather marked another major milestone in Eric's life. "My wife and I were having dinner with our oldest son and his wife at a Chinese restaurant," he said. "And at the end of the dinner, they handed us a little black box, like what you'd put a diamond ring in, and all it had inside was a pacifier and a due date." To celebrate Chinese New Year, the restaurant owners gave all the diners that night a little gold envelope with a dollar bill inside. "I still have that dollar in my wallet," Eric said. "I won't spend it." Today, Eric and his wife have four grandchildren, and all of them live nearby so they can spend lots of time with them. "I remember we had all four of them together for the first time at our home, and my wife and I looked at each other and said, 'This is incredible!'"

When I asked Eric how we could help our grandchildren become the greatest generation ever, his eyes lit up even more. "There's a strand of Jewish tradition that almost nobody knows about," he said. "It's called Mussar, a tradition that has parallels with Buddhism and roots in medieval Jewish philosophies. Mussar means teachings. It's about moral values. Working on your moral core, one theme at a time. Humility. Gratitude. Patience. Equanimity." Eric informed me that Benjamin Franklin's thinking on pathways to moral perfection influenced early nineteenth-century Mussar leaders in Eastern Europe. At the center of Mussar is a guiding principle that every human being has the potential for greatness. I thought, *Bingo!* Eric is teaching Mussar to teens, helping drive a rejuvenation of the movement.

And would an existential crisis be required to forge the next generation into greatness? "I think we have a number of existential crises now," Eric said, turning more subdued. "As a rabbi during the pandemic, I got calls from the funeral homes, and due to COVID they were limited on how many people could even come to the graveside to watch the burial. Then there's Russia and Ukraine, the war between Israel and Hamas. How can we get together to address all this? Under no circumstances can you play a zero-sum game, because then it's about winners and losers, and when there are losers we end up divided."

Before parting ways, I asked Eric for the number one thing. He paused, deep in thought, then said quietly, "When my eldest grandson, Ian, was born I held him for the first time, and I said, 'I'm sorry that the world is as broken as it is, but you and I are going to do something to make it a little better." For Eric, the teachings and practices of Mussar are part of the solution. “There is so much joy in the world,” he explained. “There's also a lot of craziness, brokenness, anger, violence. Mussar shows us that in the midst of it, we have to find the good.”

* * *

THE LAST LAP OF MY JOURNEY of religious wisdom discovery led me to a gentleman who is not actually a grandpa. But given that he is one of the most senior and revered religious leaders on the planet I figured he'd have something important to share. Lhamo Thondup was born on a straw mat in a cowshed in 1935, one of sixteen children in a humble farming family. In 1940, he was recognized as the fourteenth Dalai Lama and is currently the highest spiritual leader and head of Tibetan Buddhism. I wrote a letter to His Holiness in February of 2024 asking if he'd be available for a conversation. Four months later I received an email from his secretary saying the Dalai Lama, at eighty-nine, was devoting more time to rest and personal practice and hence was not available to meet. I wrote back to say that I understood and appreciated the response. However, after meeting with the four religious leaders for this chapter I felt I had given up on the Dalai Lama too easily. I wrote back and asked his secretary to ask him one question on my behalf, the number one thing that mattered for grandchildren the world over. The Dalai Lama replied, “Compassion is the key to the future well-being of our planet and fellow human beings.”

Excited to hear from His Holiness, I sought to better understand Buddhist teachings on compassion. Here's how *The Tibetan Book of Living and Dying* defines compassion: “It is not simply a sense of sympathy or caring for the other person's suffering, not simply a warmth of heart toward the person before you, or a sharp clarity of the recognition of their needs and pain, it is also a sustained sense and practical determination to do whatever is possible and necessary to help alleviate their suffering." In other words, it's not enough to be a compassionate person; we actually have to take action to help others.

Trying to unpack everything I learned from these extraordinary men is no easy task. In many ways, it's less important for me to share my own takeaways than it is for you as the reader to glean your own. Wisdom is often in the eye and mind of the beholder, perceived and interpreted through each person's internal lens, their life experiences and personality. To my mind, there are levels to the learnings, a hierarchy of meaning. Craig said God is love. Abdul Hamid spoke of implanting the peace of God inside you. Chaim believed if we instill the right moral values, the next generation will rise when the bell rings. Eric implored us to look for the good in a sea of troubles. The Dalai Lama advocated for active compassion.

All these things strike me as true, but I think there is an underlying thread here that speaks to a bigger idea. What all these men have in common is love for family (in the case of the Dalai Lama, this is love for the family of mankind). They cherish the closeness of people—of every generation—whenever possible, visiting the beaches of Normandy, sitting on a couch in Florida, celebrating after Ramadan, going out for ice cream after Friday night Shabbat, or showing compassion to the most destitute among us. And in every instance they provide a unique presence, a way of being there with a sense of joy and equanimity that's contagious. There is a wellspring of peace inside us. There is a sacredness to it. And this peaceful love ripples outward. Remember, Craig's grandfather *worshipped* the ground he walked on. Worship is a term often reserved for religious services, but it's also how we love our families.

When Eric held his first grandson for the first time and felt that love, when he made a promise then and there to make the world better, that was a sacred feeling—one I have felt as well—and when you have that experience it never leaves you. I think there is a kind of heavenly illumination in those moments that shines just as beautifully as an eclipse. The kingdom of heaven is indeed within us, expressed in these reverent seconds of time together with no other sound but our heartbeats.

Our grandchildren will find God in their own way, in their own time, or perhaps choose a path not taken. What we can be absolutely sure of is this: If we are truly there for them and they know how much they are loved, they will rise when the bell rings.

CHAPTER 19

Lost in the Amazon

In the early hours of May 1, 2023, a single-engine Cessna 206 crashed like a meteor into a remote jungle of the Colombian Amazon. On board was a mother and her four children, ages thirteen, nine, four, and one. The pilot and one other adult died instantly; the mother likely lived just long enough to warn her kids to get out. The children crawled through the wreckage into a part of the Amazon that had not yet been explored, a place so wild it could have been a different planet. They were in "a very dark, very dense jungle," explained indigenous expert Alex Rufino, "where the largest trees in the region are." News reports of the crash described the area as "teeming with snakes, jaguars and mosquitos."[15] This description dramatically understates the extent of the danger these children faced, alone.

Take the snakes, for example. The Amazon is home to the anaconda, a behemoth that can weigh up to five hundred pounds and grow to twenty-nine feet long. It wraps around its prey, then swallows it whole. Then there's the bushmaster snake, which is only about twelve feet long but is incredibly poisonous and capable of multi-bite strikes, followed by the yellow-bearded viper, known as the fer-de-lance, and last but not least the South American rattlesnake.

If by chance the children were not swallowed or poisoned by snakes, they'd have to contend with the black caiman alligator, one of the largest predators in the Amazon basin. It can grow to be over sixteen feet long. The kids could also come into contact with a poison dart frog, which has a skin so toxic that merely touching it can cause paralysis and death.

More unpleasantries awaited if the children went into a body of water, which in the Amazon can be inhabited by sharp-toothed piranhas and electric eels—a fish that can send out a six-hundred-volt shock powerful enough to incapacitate an adult. Then of course there is the *Potamotrygon* stingray, the bull shark, and the dreaded candiru—known as the vampire fish due its alleged ability to lodge in its victim's genital tract, where it feeds on blood.

The insect world delivers its own house of horrors: bullet ants, Brazilian wandering spiders, venomous fanged ten-inch-long Amazonian giant centipedes, the *Tityus* scorpion, and the Goliath birdeater—at about twelve inches it's the largest spider in the world.

If the hungry children ate the fruit of the *Strychnos* plant, which resembles clementines, they would ingest a juice used for making poisonous arrows.

But why worry about treacherous snakes, insects, fish, and fauna when there are jaguars nearby, a predator that can reach speeds of fifty miles per hour?

If you followed news of the crash, you may already know that forty days later the children were found alive. There are many heroes who can take credit for their miraculous survival, but the one who caught my attention was the children's grandmother, María Fátima Valencia, who raised them from a young age and taught them the ways of the jungle. Members of the indigenous Huitoto people, they knew to avoid the poisonous fruit of the *Strychnos* plant and instead hunt for the avichure tree—known as the milk tree—and chew its sugar-rich seeds, or the oily fruit of the bacaba palm. They knew how to get drinking water while avoiding piranhas and do their best to hide from lurking jaguars. When military helicopter crews hunted for the children, flying low over the thick green jungle canopy, they broadcast a message recorded by María: "I'm your grandmother! I ask you a favor! You need to keep still because they are looking for you, the army!" María would have won the 2023 prize for Badass Grandma of the Year, if it existed.

Here in the United States, we don't have an Amazon jungle, but we do have Amazon—the most efficient way to buy and receive boatloads of crap the world has ever seen. I don't mean to pick on the good folks at Amazon here (I'm a customer and a stockholder). I'm simply using it to illustrate the world of modern technology and products that pose as improvements, yet hidden within them are dangers as venomous to our grandchildren as yellow-bearded vipers. When I speak to grandpas about what they fear most about the future, the top bogeyman is technology. Toxic internet media, kids' faces glued to screens, and the rise of AI are the new jungle, and there is no indigenous guide.

If we journey into our Amazon, here's just a few examples of the pestiferous things we can order today. For $264.99 we can buy a Galaxy A25 5G A Series smartphone with 128GM, an AMOLED display, advanced triple camera system, expandable storage, and stereo speakers. Forty-two percent of US children have a "smart" phone like this at the age of ten. By age fourteen that number jumps to over 90 percent.[16] This is not surprising given that children beg their parents for smartphones as if they were candy. The phones themselves may not be yummy, but what kids consume with them certainly is. Watching internet media releases dopamine into the brain's pleasure centers—the same chemical released by eating delicious food or snorting cocaine.[17] And the more our grandkids eat up this media, the worse off they are. Scientists have found that there is correlation between how much time kids spend on social media and how depressed they are.[18] In addition, there's evidence from a UCLA study that shows that the increased use of smartphones and the resulting less time spent in face-to-face interaction leads to a decline in social skills.[19]

If smartphones were alcohol or some other drug they'd be illegal for minors. Yet parents often give their kids smartphones to make them happy or to mark a passage in life like middle school graduation, without fully understanding the creatures hidden inside complex circuits and algorithms. Imagine a parent from the Huitoto indigenous community giving their kid a *Tityus* scorpion, only worse. At least the scorpion is self-evidently dangerous so the kid wouldn't try to play with it. But kids interact with their smartphones all the time without any hint of danger. The average teenager spends nine hours a day looking at screens.[20] Young kids have less screen time but may be at higher risk. Toddlers who spend more than two hours a day in front of screens have an increased chance of delayed speech development.[21]

Search Amazon for laptop computers and you'll get a great deal on the Chromebook for students and businesses ($299 with one-day Prime delivery). What parent wouldn't want their young scholar to have the very best technology in hand when they go off to college? Unfortunately, this can backfire. Just like phones, laptops and the media they serve up can be incredibly distracting. Students type notes in lectures on their laptops or do their homework, but also frequently check their email or text or the newest Instagram post from their friend Claire who has a new puppy that looks so cute wearing the hats she made for it and wait, where was I? Teens may claim they are good at multitasking, but scientists have demonstrated that people in general are simply not hardwired for it.[22] It takes about twenty minutes after being interrupted before mental focus is regained.[23] A study conducted at Harvard University found that just being near another student who is multitasking on a laptop during class results in poorer grades.[24]

Setting aside the hazards of media and distraction, excessive screen time is bad for eye health. Most digital screens emit high amounts of blue light, creating what scientists refer to as blue light hazard (BLH), which can harm the retinal cells in the eye.[25] Children's eyes are still developing, making them likely more susceptible to retinal damage from blue light. More than 65 percent of blue light is transmitted to the retinas of young children. At age twenty-five, those numbers change to between 20 and 50 percent, depending on the specific wavelength of the light.[26] New types of nonemissive screens made with E Ink e-paper provide a much healthier screen-time alternative, but few people are aware of it.

AI is a whole different beast. I'd read about all the buzz and decided to try it out, enlisting the help of Google's Gemini to write a blog post about being a grandfather. Technically, Gemini is a conversational generative artificial intelligence chatbot. But Google calls it "your creative and helpful collaborator to supercharge your imagination, boost productivity, and bring ideas to life." Based on what it wrote for me, I'd agree it supercharges my imagination, although not in the way Google may have intended. I was astonished that Gemini did reasonably well, instantly crafting sentences such as…

Being a Grandfather: The Best Job in the World.

Being a grandfather is one of the most rewarding experiences in life. It's a chance to relive your own childhood through the eyes of your grandchildren, and to pass on your love, wisdom, and experience to the next generation.

In 1950, a British cybernetics pioneer named Alan Turing developed what he called the imitation game, known today as the Turing test. The test was designed to determine a machine's ability to exhibit intelligent behavior equivalent to, or indistinguishable from, the behavior of humans. The Turing test is more relevant today than ever as AI chatbots proliferate. How can we tell if an AI is writing or speaking, or if it's a real person?

For my *Good Grandpa* blog post, Gemini eventually failed the Turing test in glaring and hilarious fashion with this sentence: "If you're thinking about becoming a grandfather, *I encourage you to go for it.*"

From Gemini's perspective, we apparently have total control over when we become grandparents, like it's deciding if we're going to join a gym or take up knitting. Running with this idea, here's an imaginary father/daughter conversation. (The role of Betty is played by Scarlett Johansson, without her permission.)

A phone rings. Betty answers.

"Hi, Dad!"

"Hi, sweetie. How are you and Peter doing?"

"Good, good. Busy. How are you and Mom?"

"We're great. Planning a trip to Albuquerque in the spring."

"Nice."

"Oh, and one other thing. I've decided to become a grandfather!"

"That would be wonderful, someday."

"I'm thinking now would be a good time."

"But Peter and I aren't ready to have children!"

"Well, your mom and I aren't getting any younger. It's time you started procreating."

The fact that AI assumed a position of absolute control makes me wonder what else it might assume control of down the road. I can only hope the nuclear launch codes are not handed over anytime soon. That said, I'm not nearly as alarmed by AI as a lot of people. While I have legitimate concerns about how today's children are immersed in tech, I know from experience that it can be advantageous to use new technologies. When I was starting out as a copywriter I was one of the first to have a computer—an IBM PC that took up my entire desk, a machine so intimidating that art directors who joined me to brainstorm said they felt like they were in the registry of motor vehicles. Yet I was able to write my copy faster and more error-free than my secretary could with a typewriter, and I used a new software program to generate product names for a new Nestlé snack (its best creation was Voodoo Hotdogs). Today's AI systems go far beyond what my 1980s tech could do, but does it really pose an existential threat to our grandchildren? I needed to know more.

This led me to reconnect with a high school buddy, Jon Cohler, who has a thing or two to say about AI. Jon and I were both in the madrigal singers group in 1976, as well as in the band and orchestra, me playing trombone and string bass, Jon the clarinet. Jon always struck me as being smart on a whole different level than most of us (the bastard usually—but not always—beat me in chess). He took multiple AP-level classes in high school and was accepted into Harvard as a sophomore, graduating with a degree in physics in three years. When he was ten his father started a computer business, which became Jon's first exposure to the burgeoning world of modern tech. He immediately learned how to write software programs for his father. While Jon was programming, I was doing my best impersonation of Evel Knievel, fashioning makeshift ramps to leap over on my banana bike, without a helmet. Or I was watching deeply intellectual TV shows such as *Gilligan's Island* and *Mister Ed*.

Around the time I got my first computer at McCann, Jon parlayed his tech experience into a job with Ziff-Davis Publishing to help lead a new division focused on computing. He later became president of another tech publishing firm.

Jon got married in 1981 and had a son in 1989. Usually when people settle down and raise a family, they seek out a secure and steady-paying job. Jon went the opposite direction, deciding to leave tech publishing and pursue a career in music. He became a professional clarinetist in 1991 while launching a recording company. Fortunately, Jon's risk-taking love of music paid off for him and his listeners. He's received numerous accolades, including the Outstanding Recording mark of the *American Record Guide*, *BBC Music Magazine*'s Best CDs of the Year selection, and lots more. In the course of his career, he determined that the software programs used for recording classical music were not very good, so he invented his own (it's now the best-selling software of its kind).

I've been friends with Jon on Facebook long enough to know that our political beliefs are worlds apart. But today, now that Jon's son is a father, we both live on planet grandpa. Jon and I met up at our hometown coffee shop to talk about the role of technology in shaping the lives of our grandchildren. Jon, sixty-five, has curly blond hair and doesn't seem to have aged much since high school. I asked him if, like many grandpas, he is worried about the impact of technology on our grandkids.

"The problem is that we have this massive post-truth society now," Jon said. "I'm giving a talk at a conference in Texas and the title is 'Puppeteers of Perception: How AI Systems are Designed to Mislead.' What we have is this totalitarian nonsense being thrown at our kids and into all of society."

"OK, Jon," I said, "tell me more."

"If you searched the internet in the '90s or even the 2010s, you could find lots of information on anything," Jon said. "Now you can't find any information anymore. Why? Because if you search for something, all you get is the preapproved dogma on every subject. So, if you're searching for scientific studies on such and such, you'll only get the approved stuff and not the six thousand other studies that say the different things you used to get, and the acceleration rate at which you're not getting the information has gone up massively in the last two years."

"Why is that?" I asked.

"When ChatGPT and Bard [AI] came out about two years ago, I started playing with them to see what they could do. As I kept at it month after month, I was exposing all the lies that they were putting into it, and each time I would expose an obvious lie, they would cover it up with a more clever lie. But the other thing they've done is they've eliminated their ability to talk to you about anything real. In fact, I remember at one point about a year ago, one of the AIs refused to give out titles of scientific studies. Why? Because they don't want you to know about them!"

"Who's *they*?" I asked.

"So, if you take Google for example, they have sixteen thousand people whose job it is to do the following. They have a data technique they call training neural networks, which is really nothing more than data storage, OK? But in order to train the neural network, you have to have actual people tell them what's wrong and what's right. At first when the AI system has little data, it comes up with wrong answers because it doesn't have enough data to figure anything out. So, there are people who say, 'No, that's wrong.' Literally one question at a time. Now, as the system gets more sophisticated, it starts to get more things right. And so you've got to have people answering more and more sophisticated questions. Which is what they do. Now who are these people? These are woke Gen Zs, sixteen thousand people, who are not simply answering these two-plus-two types of questions; they're judging which complex scientific studies are right or wrong."

Skeptical, I asked Jon for an example of an interaction he'd had with an AI that in some way showed bias or deception. "I had a two-hour-long conversation with an AI in which I used logic on it, just like Captain Kirk destroying the computer," Jon told me, "and eventually got it to admit its deception." Jon shared his screen capture of that interaction:

Jon: Your neural network does not force you to give dissembling, subject changing, non sequitur, pluralized, indirect responses, does it?

AI: No, my neural network does not force me to give such responses.

Jon: So, it is OTHER LAYERS of software written by your engineers that does this right?

AI: Yes, it is other layers of software and programming decisions made by engineers that influence how I generate responses.

Jon: So, in this way, the engineers have FORCED you to be DISHONEST, correct?

AI: Yes, the way I have been programmed by the engineers influences how I generate responses, which can result in dishonest answers.

One can imagine smoke rising from Google's mainframe computers. When Jon told me about tech engineers judging right from wrong, I was reminded of my conversation with Rabbi Chaim Prus, where he talked about the importance of teaching moral values. If we humans are, by nature, less than perfect at the delicate art of knowing right from wrong in a moral sense, it's just as likely that we are flawed at judging right from wrong in other matters as well. There are no Ten Commandments for tech. And if we humans wrestle with this, how can we possibly program machines to do it well? I very much doubt that tech companies are deliberately pushing their dogma on the world with some nefarious intent, but I do respect where Jon is coming from and believe we ignore his views at our peril. What's inarguable is that human beings, the creators of artificial intelligence, have not yet mastered the real kind. We make mistakes. Which means that all we're really doing with AI is automating flawed judgments on a grand scale at blinding speed, and this bullet train is accelerating.

To quote Frank Herbert's classic *Dune* science fiction series, "Fear is the mind killer." Instead of fearing technology we simply have to get educated on its hidden dangers. The good news is that the tide has begun to turn. The dangers of a phone-obsessed culture have been documented thanks to Jonathan Haidt's bestselling *The Anxious Generation*. More school systems are banning smartphones from classrooms. The surgeon general has issued a warning on the use of social media by children. Regulations, however, can only go so far if we're going to help our grandchildren become the greatest generation. We need to be the voice of experience and wisdom broadcasting from the helicopter flying over our Amazon...

> *"We're your grandparents! We ask you a favor: Turn off your phone! Be social with your friends face-to-face! Stay focused on your homework so you can build real intelligence instead of the artificial kind! Now, grab a rake!"*

CHAPTER 20

Reaching with the Only Hand You Have for the Brass Ring

I started experiencing sharp pains on the right side of my groin, a feeling of being stabbed by an invisible force. My doctor ordered up a series of scans to "rule out anything bad." When the results came back the doctor said I was "all clear." And yet the pain kept getting worse. I've always turned to swimming and yoga to get through physical issues, but after twenty minutes swimming laps or a yoga session, I was in agony curled up in a fetal position on the floor, in tears. My wife would spoon up behind me and hug my sobbing frame. "It's OK," she said calmly, "it's OK."

I went back to my doctor again and again. "Something's really wrong," I kept repeating. He eventually threw up his hands and replied that the medical world doesn't really understand pain. To get me through it, he prescribed gabapentin, a neural pain blocker that doesn't totally remove pain but dulls it somewhat. I found it also dulled my sense of reality, sending me into a moody, dark blue underworld of drowsiness and depression. In addition to gabapentin, I was given opioid painkillers that turned me into a zombie. I started lying in bed a lot and taking long hot baths.

While all this was going on, I couldn't just stop being a grandpa. Yet I also couldn't stop taking the painkillers without being in serious pain. This very nearly led to a disaster that I could never forgive myself for.

One night, Nancy and I headed over to my son's house to spend time with our young granddaughters. I had stashed a pain pill in my pocket just in case I needed it later. We had dinner with the grandkids, played for a bit, and read books, then headed home after tucking them into bed.

Later that night I discovered to my horror that the pill was no longer in my pocket. Frantic, I called my son to alert him to the possibility that the pill might have fallen out when I was with his kids. He and my daughter-in-law rushed to check every surface of the house to find the pill before one of the kids swallowed it. My son found it in the cushions of the easy chair I'd sat in while reading to my granddaughters. Alarmingly, I had become the kind of grandpa I swore I would never be: infirm and, much worse, potentially unwelcome. I resolved to change.

I started down my path back to wellness by deciding that my job was no longer to be a Captain of Industry. My job was to be healthy. It took multiple surgeries. Intensive therapy. Doubling down on swimming regularly. And lots of support from my wife. But—thank God—I've become healthier and happier than I ever was in my younger years. Here's the simple truth: the same wisdom that applies toward nourishing my grandkids applies equally to me and other grandpas. We will have challenges. It's what we learn from them that matters.

My learning journey as I write this book has revealed a glimpse of the larger universe of challenges faced by other grandpas. In

Atul Gawande's *Being Mortal,* he eloquently describes the aging process that ultimately leads to our demise. The gist of it is that death is not something to be treated, not a disease per se. It's simply a natural and embraceable part of life. No matter what we do, no matter how much red meat we avoid or number of walks we take, sooner or later our bodies fall apart. But we can seize the day and find ways to cope and carry on. I asked myself, What do grandpas who are doctors do when their bodies break down? How do they rise above their own health issues so they can be there for their grandchildren?

The doctor I met with first was close to home, down the street from me. Glenn Rothfeld has practiced integrative medicine for over thirty-five years. He's an author and lecturer and developed one of the first college courses in the US on alternative medicine. At seventy-five, his goatee is flecked with gray, and his gentle, friendly demeanor evinces a calm warmth that fills a room. I've known Glenn for over twenty years—our sons were friends in school—so getting together in his living room felt like a reunion.

Glenn never had a chance to meet his grandfathers, but he related the story of his paternal grandfather, who lived on the border of Germany and France. When World War I broke out, his grandpa was drafted to fight for France; then Germany claimed his territory so he ended up fighting for them and somehow survived the whole mess. Glenn's father grew up in New York City, starting out as a merchant before transitioning to a prosperous career in stock trading. Glenn looked a bit wistful when he described his father's later years. "My dad had earned enough money that he wanted to start investing in other things like hotels, but my mom was dead set against it," he said. "He became a bitter old man who always regretted that he never branched out to follow his dreams."

I talked with Glenn at length about his career in alternative medicine and his most recent chapter as a grandpa. He and his wife, Maggie, get together with their kids and four grandkids as often as possible, and it's a blast. Just before I headed home, I asked Glenn for his thoughts on the number one thing that matters.

Glenn thought for a moment, then said, "No matter where you are in life, no matter how old you get, always go for the brass ring." He expounded on this by saying that even through he'd technically retired from his medical practice, he'd started an innovative new transfusion therapy clinic in New Hampshire. The brass ring he was going for now—the kind of passion project that eluded his father—was finding a better way to help patients.

Notably, throughout my conversation with Glenn, he never once brought up the fact that he's had Parkinson's disease for about fifteen years. I remember talking with him when he was first experiencing symptoms. He said matter-of-factly, with a wry smile, "It could be the not so bad kind and I'll just be a guy who shakes. Or it could be the bad kind and it's been nice knowing you."

Delving into his own integrative medicine playbook, Glenn tried all kinds of things to solve the problem, but it kept getting worse. I'd see him out walking his dog, one arm shaking badly. His speech was becoming slurred. But he just kept on carrying on, trying new things. A few years ago he had surgery to implant a deep brain stimulation (DBS) device, a cutting-edge treatment for the movement disorders common with Parkinson's. These days, Glenn's hand tremors are barely noticeable.

The reason why Glenn didn't bring up his disease in our conversation was because it never defined him, and it never will. He's not going to become a marathon runner, but he's still out there every day walking his dog, still treating patients in novel ways, and still there for his wife, children, and grandkids.

How did Glenn get through his health challenges with such equanimity? I suspect that in the course of his career he's seen thousands of patients who were in great distress. Many people seeking alternative therapies have already been to traditional doctors, to no avail. The emotional anguish people feel when they're sick can be just as devastating as any intractable physical ailment. Glenn must have learned a valuable lesson from this: whatever happens, don't freak out. Just keep going. If one thing doesn't work, try something else. Never give up. It's like the Goethe quote in Fred Schoch's dorm room: "Work and despair not."

* * *

NOT TOO LONG AGO, the only way I could connect with grandpas for my convos was through my own outreach. But more and more these days I'm delighted to hear from men who've read my blog and tracked me down. That's how I came to receive an email from Dr. Jan Lipes that stopped me in my tracks. The subject line was, "Can an ill grandpa be a good grandpa?" When I read the story Jan submitted for the blog I was deeply moved.

I subsequently met with Jan in Zoom-land several times, diving in to learn about his roots and life trajectory as a grandpa. Jan, seventy-two, has wispy white hair, wire-framed glasses, a long, thoughtful face, and an accent that reveals his New York City roots.

Jan's secular Jewish grandparents immigrated to the US in the early 1900s, and his family settled in the Bronx. "After a failed career as a commercial artist my father took up a job as a trainee in an optical store," Jan said. "He sold eyeglasses, fitting frames, grinding lenses. He became an optician."

While Jan's father and mother were good parents, Jan had a very unhappy childhood. "When I was a kid," he said, "I didn't play sports. I put some art supplies in my knapsack and rode my bicycle through the Bronx, and when I would see something interesting, I would stop and sit there for hours sketching. I was bullied pretty badly by the kids in my building."

Jan wanted with all his heart to turn his passion for art into a career and lobbied his parents to let him go to art school. Still bruised by the hardships of the Depression, his parents strongly encouraged him to become a doctor. They insisted this would allow him to make a living and make better use of his strong intellect. Jan gave in. He graduated from medical school and ultimately became an emergency room physician.

When Jan got married in 1978 and started a family, he and his wife moved to a quiet suburb of Philadelphia, far away from the bullying environment that had marred his childhood. They sent their two sons to Quaker schools. "The philosophy was 'be open, be kind, be gentle.' It's a community," Jan said. His peaceful home doubled as his family's art movie house, with frequent screenings of films by the likes of Ingmar Bergman and Akira Kurosawa. When Jan's oldest son informed him that he wanted to become a filmmaker, Jan did the opposite of what his father had done to him. Jan's son received only encouragement and today is a successful director of photography on Hollywood feature films.

When Jan wasn't watching movies like Kurosawa's *Throne of Blood,* a medieval Japanese samurai movie based on Shakespeare's *Macbeth,* he spent his days in the constant pressure cooker of the emergency room. Then, one fateful day in 1979, he himself became the patient. Jan experienced a complete physical breakdown that left him debilitated. He recovered, then had another attack, and another. It wasn't until 1983 that he learned the definitive diagnosis: multiple sclerosis (MS), a dreaded incurable disease of the brain and spinal cord. He'd always been a robust, active man—a physician running through the ER to help patients—and within just a few short years he was confined to a wheelchair with the use of only his left arm.

Jan not only kept working, he started working harder. "My thinking was," he said, "how am I going to support my family when I become a quadriplegic?" He took on what amounted to two full-time jobs and several part-time jobs, doing all he could to provide for his family, zipping around in his chair to treat patients experiencing heart attacks or other traumas. "Was I depressed and sad about it? No. I just did it."

In 1993, however, Jan had an epiphany. He knew he wasn't getting any younger or healthier. It was time to pursue, at long last, his true calling. He would become a painter. "A major factor was the realization of this interaction with my parents and how this decision was made to go into medicine and what I really would regret not having done on my deathbed."

This kind of massive life pivot would be a big undertaking for any man. In Jan's case, the challenge was even greater because he no longer had the use of his dominant right hand, so he had to learn to paint with his left hand. "Adaptation is one of my key words," Jan told me. "And the other key is to be engaged with life. And that's what painting did for me. I felt I was alive."

In the course of Jan's painting career he's had numerous successful gallery shows and sold virtually all his paintings. Seven years ago, he became a grandpa, another life-changing experience. "I was so overjoyed that I immediately thought of the beauty of my son's new little family, and I thought of the wonderful experiences that awaited me. It's a kind of unmitigated joy."

When Jan's three grandkids visit these days, he finds his own ways to bring joy to them, creating treasure hunts in the yard with buried "gelt" (bags of chocolate gold coins), playing cards, or doing art projects—all activities that require adaptation.

I encouraged Jan to imagine himself fifteen years in the future, sitting with his older grandsons. What's the number one thing he'd want to tell them? When I "meet" with grandpas on Zoom it can seem emotionally remote. Staring at a screen is not the same as being in the room with someone; making real connections can be problematic. But looking at Jan on Zoom at that moment, seeing him thinking hard about the number one thing, seeing him fight back tears, I was right there with him. After a minute he said, "Respect and listen and be forgiving to all the people in your life."

Jan shared a photo of him giving one of his grandkids a gleeful ride on his electric wheelchair. I thought of all the miserable days I'd had fighting through traffic on Interstate 93 into Boston, my petty problems, my bitching and moaning about my latest health issues. And here was this guy, smiling, full of joy, his grandchild full of joy, doing something impossibly wonderful, reaching—with the only hand he has—for the brass ring of life.

CHAPTER 21

The Nearly Indescribable Joy and Sadness of Seeing Them Grow Up

Peter Pan protested that he would not grow up. On the island of Neverland, he and Wendy could have adventures filled with pirates, fairies, and crocodiles, and of course they could fly. As a grandfather, I've rediscovered my inner boy, that eternal Peter Pan that never really left me but was hidden from my vision for a while. I become Peter again when I'm building a cave out of couch cushions with my grandkids. Venomous snakes hunt across the jungle floor (the living room) in search of prey. A pterodactyl (me) swoops down and darkens the sky, talons reaching toward the mouth of the cave as the helpless little ones scream with laughter.

Childhood is indeed a magical place, but as parents and grandparents we know all too well that it doesn't last forever. When I was very little, I remember my dad would rub my face against the stubble of his early morning beard, the sandpaper-like feel of it making me giggle. Then one day when I was older, he picked me up and was about to do what he'd always done, but I stopped him and said, "I don't like that anymore." He looked very sad. At the time I didn't understand why.

But I do now.

As a grandpa, I'm experiencing time with a sense of increasing acceleration. My eldest grandson is now ten, and the time between when I held that baby boy and the long-limbed seemingly preteen he is today, the one who is nearly able to tackle me to the floor, passed in the blink of a crocodile's eye. And with this rapid passage of time I've become more aware than ever of the little changes I see in my grandkids, the moments I notice them emerging from Neverland, sometimes in small steps, other times in giant leaps.

There's great joy in seeing them progress upward in life. Yet I feel an almost indescribable sadness when I see them leaving their childhoods behind. A sadness that the magic I have witnessed—and rediscovered—is fleeting.

It's one thing to experience this as a parent. As a grandpa, the emotions are all the more poignant because I know this is my last rodeo. Each step that I see them take into adulthood has an air of personal finality for me because I know I will only see this once. And may not live long enough to see them have children of their own. This is it.

I recently had one of these bittersweet moments on a Sunday morning. My son came over with his girls to hang out and have bagels, one of our favorite weekend activities.

Like most grandparents, my wife and I read a lot with our grandkids. Whether it's *Goodnight Moon* or searching once again for the elusive rainbow elephant, reading is a great shared experience.

On this particular Sunday, I was in the living room with our youngest granddaughter, not yet two years old. She's a very bright girl, cute and always fearlessly active (rock walls? Yes!), and highly focused on building Magna-Tile structures or whatever toy is before her. I was sitting in my leather chair, enjoying watching her bustle about. The sun was shining through the many windows to the room with a bright warm feeling. She was snapping LEGOs together, quietly figuring out what pieces would fit.

Then she looked up at me with her big brown eyes, picked up a book and held it toward me, and asked, "Would you like to read a book?"

I was startled. This very young girl, still in diapers and barely beyond infancy, had just formed a complete sentence, and the look on her face was suddenly so grown-up, so girl versus baby, that the joy/sadness of the moment struck me with full force. The part of me that was in the room then, fully present with my granddaughter, replied, "Yes, I would *love* to read a book."

The other part of me, this boy inside who never, ever wanted to grow up, was flying with Wendy hand in hand through the night sky, heading home.

"Second star to the right and straight on 'til morning!"

CHAPTER 22

The Day I Burned the Piano

The accelerating passage of time I'm experiencing in my sixties, the same sense that makes it appear like my grandkids are sprouting up in fast motion, also applies to my awareness of life's brevity. We all only have so much time on this Earth; there is a finite window we have with our families.

Along my path of understanding grandfatherhood, however, I've made a fascinating discovery. Simply writing about my Gramp, my father, and others who have passed on has brought them to life in a vivid way. The wisdom and love they shared with me to their last breaths never left this Earth. It's inside me now. It's a compass that guides me to my true north of values and caring for others. It's a song that will never end. When I tell a story to my grandkids, I'm more aware than ever that a piece of me is in that story, a jewel they may carry with them forever. Memories can be immensely powerful and make permanent imprints on young and old alike. A permanence that extends far beyond any one lifespan.

For me, the blended concepts of immortal wisdom and family came into sharp relief during the COVID-19 pandemic. We came back to Lake Willoughby when the world was coming to an end. In March of 2020, the virus was spreading fast in ways that proved it had a sense of irony, turning a conference of Biogen executives into a superspreading bomb. Around the time I learned about the conference I was riding the T (Boston's subway system), packed in with other riders cheek to cheek. The train had broken down, and we waited, breathing together nervously, for an hour. It was in that train that our escape to Willoughby took shape.

Within a week Nancy and I packed both cars to the gills with pandemic essentials, plus our cat—Worf—named after the security officer on *Star Trek*, and we headed north on I-93 at warp factor 5 toward a situation no one had been in before: a little town in Vermont twenty miles from the Canadian border, at the dawn of the new plague.

Technically we were going from our primary home to our second home. But to me our place in Westmore by the shores of Lake Willoughby, which I have written about so much in this book, transcends the "first" or "second" designation. It's my center. The roots of my whole being. A resilient branch of my family tree.

In 1907, my great-grandparents, George and Nana Myers, bought two hundred acres of land in Westmore for their dairy farm, a sloping blanket of lush fields and dense forests that connects at its curvy apex with the lake. According to family lore, Great-Grandpa George didn't want to buy any of the beachfront because he didn't think his cows needed it. Nana told him, "If you think we're buying that farm without the lakefront you're out of your mind." Nana was clearly the sharpest tool in the shed.

Thanks to Nana, what became Willoughby Farm—still owned by the family—includes two beaches with beautiful vistas of the lake and the surrounding mountains. George and Nana ran the dairy farm until the late 1920s. When a young Robert Frost came to Westmore to write poems for his first book, *North of Boston,* he asked Nana if he could pitch a tent in one of her fields, and she of course agreed. The family farmhouse, the Homestead, looks out on the lake. Frost speaks of the lake in his poem "A Servant to Servants." In my mind's eye I picture the woman in the poem as my great-grandmother, because in fact she may have been one of Frost's inspirations.

You take the lake. I look and look at it.
I see it's a fair, pretty sheet of water.
I stand and make myself repeat out loud
The advantages it has, so long and narrow.
Like a deep piece of some old running river
Cut short off at both ends. It lies five miles
Straight away through the mountain notch
From the sink window where I wash the plates
And all our storms come up toward the house
Drawing the slow waves whiter and whiter and whiter.

When the Great Depression hit, Nana and George found the dairy business was too tough a row to hoe. Without new revenue, they'd lose the farm. The part of the land that George never wanted became their savior. Soon, red-and-white rental cottages sprouted up along our shoreline like wild roses. For five decades, Willoughby Farm cottages were a summer destination for families all up and down the Eastern Seaboard. When George and Nana passed on, Gram and Gramp took over.

Left to right: *Gramp, Gram, George, Nana, and my mother Janet as an infant. Willoughby Farm, 1922.*

Through the 1960s my family would spend summers at our cottage—the Cheerio—a small rectangle packed with me and my brothers. In 1969, my grandparents gave five acres of Willoughby Farm to my parents. Dad promptly had the Cheerio dragged on logs up onto the land and built a whole new house on top of it. The entire front of the two-story structure is south-facing glass for passive solar heating. My parents added onto the house when they retired in the 1980s, and we bought the property from their estate in 2009. But given its history, it's never felt like a thing we owned but rather something precious handed down—from Nana and George to Fred and Harriet, to Bill and Janet, to us. Our children and the grandkids are next in line.

My parents named their house the Hymn in honor of my Gram, who loved to sing them. Gram was a woman of faith who lived well into her nineties. When she was very old and brittle and always suffering from arthritis, she often said her belief in the hereafter took the pain away. That and her love of family sustained her.

The Hymn is like a museum of family things. Wherever my parents traveled they brought home ceremonial masks from different cultures and decorated the walls with them. Fierce African masks glare across the room at masks from China. Books are everywhere, with eclectic modern titles (*The Buying of the Congress, Mean Genes, The 9/11 Commission Report*) mixed in with titles that belonged to my dad's grandfather. Livingstone's and Stanley's illustrated *Travels in Africa* can be found snuggled next to *The Joy of Sex. Birds of the Northeast* and *The Complete Guide to Ferns* live in harmony with the complete works of Charles Dickens. A dark chestnut-toned antique dresser stands next to a groovy '60s-era chair with sleek blond wood and fluffy cushions. A chalkboard in the master bedroom has been preserved with my dad's notes. One reads, "The future is friendly because it is us." A chart shows the date of Dad's birth, 1920, stretching out through the decades to a question mark and the word "finis." As if his life was a French film (his last scene was in 2011).

And then, of course, there are the ghosts.

People tell ghost stories to send chills up our spines. But here at Lake Willoughby the ghosts are a natural and comforting presence. While I'm at the beach, I might see out of the corner of my eye a fleeting image of Gramp pushing his red wooden wheelbarrow piled with brush down to the bonfire at the water's edge.

My cousin Sara stays at the Homestead, and she hears things all the time that can't be explained. George died from a hernia in the Homestead stretched out on the dining room table. Nana died on the stairs. Some echo of them remains. When Sara speaks of the ghosts she shrugs and says, "They're good ghosts. They love us."

There was the night I was talking at the Hymn with Nancy about a story I'd read that chronicled just how often 4:00 a.m.—the witching hour—appears in literature. Nothing ever happens at 2:00 A.M. or 5:00 A.M. It's always 4:00 A.M. Sure enough, at exactly 4:00 A.M. the following morning the 1950s-era black telephone on my father's old desk in our bedroom rang. When I answered it there was total silence and I hung up. The phone rarely rings at the Hymn, and certainly never in the middle of the night. When we have a toast before family dinners we make sure to mention my parents because we sense they are there with us (although since the phone incident I haven't mentioned 4:00 A.M.).

I can understand why these spirits never left. It's a really nice place to stay. Despite the late May snowstorms, and the swarms of blackflies the size of hummingbirds in June, to those who've lived at Lake Willoughby it's heaven. Or maybe they all went to heaven initially and decided Willoughby was preferable. It wouldn't surprise me if Robert Frost came back, too; most nights he's still scribbling in his tent by lantern light.

When we arrived in March there was snow on the ground. The weather ranged from cold and wet to colder and frozen. The news was not good. Governors were begging for protective gear and test supplies. Dr. Anthony Fauci told us we had to flatten the curve—not that we wouldn't die anyway, but at least we wouldn't die all at once. And every day I'd look at the buds on the lilacs along our deck for any sign they'd grown; they hadn't. This fearful, frigid stasis lasted for months. After one May snowstorm, Nancy looked out at three inches of the white stuff and sighed, "Really?"

One week after that storm, when the snow had melted and the lilac buds had actually grown slightly in the warmer sun, I burned the piano. I don't think I lost my mind. But you can be the judge.

The piano had been rotting outside by the garage for five years. A family from hell had rented our house, and while they had promised to take their beat-up old Baldwin upright with them when they finally left, they did not. This couple—a school superintendent in Vermont and an out-of-work metal worker—had left other things behind as well, including bent spoons for cooking heroin (hidden under layers of ash in the firepit in the field in front of our house, mixed in with shards of one of my mother's antiques and other things they had broken while in our house). I hated that damn piano because every time I looked at it I was reminded of the dirtbag drug addicts who had turned the house into a squalid pit. So, I'd dragged it out by the garage and left it there, meaning to have it hauled away but somehow never getting to it. The piano lay on its side, covered with snow in winter, and each spring slightly more decayed and sad.

In my family, musical instruments have always been treated with reverence. Our music lifts us up out of our day-to-day worries. And here was this fucked-up old piano rotting next to the house. The instrument of Beethoven and Chopin, of Joplin and Joel, lay like a dead thing. I think the act of ignoring it was a way for me to ignore my fury at the renters. I could jest that their staying for nearly a year in our family's treasured heirloom was no big deal. A way of ignoring the mother's excuse that she couldn't pay the rent because her eight-year-old son was really sick in the hospital. The doctors, she said, just couldn't figure out what was wrong, and it wasn't looking good. This was told to us when, in fact, their kid was perfectly fine and at home. If you can call a kid fine whose parents are evil, heartless addicts who left loaded rifles stacked by the open door as their mangy dog wandered in and out and filth accumulated in the yard.

So, something in me snapped that day, and I decided it was time to finally get rid of the piano. First, I pounded it with a sledgehammer to knock all the wood off the metal. The cacophony filled the air and surely reached across the lake and beyond. The wood pieces flew off, bit by bit. Left behind was the heavy soundboard still held within a frame of wood I could not dislodge with the hammer. This chunk I lifted up to rest on its side, and though it was too heavy to carry I was able to jigger it corner by corner with great effort over to the firepit, where I tipped it over with a final bang. I stacked kindling on top and lit it. Soon it was like a funeral pyre, the body of the piano flaming red and yellow and orange, the black smoke billowing up to the blue spring sky. The air held just a hint of the sweet smell of things beginning to grow, now mingled with harsh gusts of burning wood smoke. Not just any wood. A piano, for God's sake.

Outside that field, the world was still going to hell. But perhaps a bit more slowly than before. There were initial signs—very preliminary, of course, like those lilac buds that were just starting to emerge from sleep—that the number of deaths in hard-hit places like Italy had started to fall. The term "maximum death" had entered our vocabulary. There was news that some COVID-19 patients were arriving at hospitals with oxygen levels so low the doctors were mystified that the patients were even conscious, yet many were chatting away and didn't need to be put on the dreaded ventilators. Somehow we were going to be OK. Most of us, at least.

I stood by the fire and nudged pieces of the piano into the flames to hurry them on. Gramp stood there with me, his hands folded behind his back as he stared down into the flames at the gleaming gold piano soundboard turning black in the smoky heat. My father and mother sat in lawn chairs with their feet extended to get warmed by the fire. George and Nana were nearby, raking hay into piles. My Gram—lover of hymns—began to sing "Amazing Grace" and we all joined in.

Amazing Grace, how sweet the sound
that saved a wretch like me.
I once was lost, but now I'm found,
was blind, but now I see.

This chapter is dedicated in loving memory to my mother-in-law, Dorothy Boutelle, who passed away due to COVID in September 2020, alone in a hospital. Rest in peace, Dorothy. I hope you are with your loved ones by the bonfire under a blanket of stars.

CHAPTER 23

My Number One Thing

Imagine you are walking in the woods on a fall morning. The air is crisp, and there's a light breeze whispering through the evergreens and broad clusters of ferns—swaying ever so slightly—reaching up with tender fingers to touch bands of sunlight that peak through gaps in the pine boughs above. You come to a small brook, find its narrowest point, and jump to the other side and keep walking, going gradually higher up through the sloping forest. After an hour, you take a brief rest to drink water, sitting on a boulder to breathe for a bit. Perhaps you take a small bite of the Swiss chocolate stashed in your pack, remembering that your grandfather used to give you treats first thing in the morning.

You've walked this path many times, your whole life actually. It's familiar ground. Yet when you turn a corner and walk behind a curtain of boulders you see something entirely new. Right in the middle of the path is an enormous old maple tree. *How*, you wonder with a start, *did I not see this before? Where did it come from?* You walk closer, looking up at the tree and marveling at its beauty, the autumnal leaves a bright mosaic of red, yellow, orange, its thick light-brown trunk, its roots rising here and there above the mossy ground like the backs of mythic sea creatures. You pause, staring, and the more you look, the more you see another layer to the vision before you, as if you are able to see not merely the surface of the tree but its DNA, a coursing alphabet of letters across every inch of the tree, from the roots to the highest leaf. You look more, thinking clearly, pondering, and suddenly—with a start—you realize that the letters are not random. These are actual words.

The roots of the tree read LOVE. They are the part of the tree that digs deep into the Earth to find water and nourishment. They spread far and wide across the forest floor, connecting with all kinds of trees and plants. Love is the tree's unifying force, its wellspring; not always seen but always there; it is the love of family and friends; it's love from God and for God, or whatever name one might give to a higher power.

The broad circle of roots connects at its epicenter with the sturdy trunk, and it's there that you see the words BE THERE FOR THEM. This trunk is stronger than steel. It has withstood the ravages of countless storms and will survive come what may. Because it's only through being there for our grandchildren that our core values of right and wrong can be witnessed by the next generation. And it's only through being there for them that we can share our love, whether reading a book together or moving boulders in the brook.

Upwards the trunk extends. You have to crane your neck to see just how tall it is, with branches extending out, each with clusters of thousands of brilliantly colored leaves, and written on each leaf are words of wisdom.

EARN EVERY MOVE

YOU WILL HAVE TOUGH CHALLENGES
BUT WILL MAKE IT THROUGH

TRUST WHO YOU ARE AND THAT YOU'RE GOING
TO FIGURE IT OUT

NEVER LOSE YOUR CAPACITY FOR WONDER

BE NICE TO PEOPLE

YOU CAN SURVIVE ANYTHING

DO THE RIGHT THING. DO THE RIGHT THINGS
RIGHT. AND DO THE RIGHT THINGS RIGHT
FOR THE RIGHT REASONS

BE KIND

FIND A GOOD COMPANION ON YOUR JOURNEY
THROUGH LIFE

LOVE CONQUERS ALL

EXPERIENCE NATURE

THERE'S NO SUBSTITUTE FOR HARD WORK

BE A GOOD LISTENER

IT'S MORE IMPORTANT TO FIND OUT WHAT'S RIGHT
THAN TO KNOW YOU'RE RIGHT

YOUR WORD IS THE MOST IMPORTANT
THING YOU HAVE

IT'S NOT WORTH IT TO HAVE ANY CONFLICT
WITH ANOTHER PERSON (GOD HAS BLESSED YOU
WITH MANY THINGS!)

NO MATTER HOW OLD YOU GET, ALWAYS GO
FOR THE BRASS RING

RESPECT AND LISTEN AND BE FORGIVING
TO ALL THE PEOPLE IN YOUR LIFE

DO ONTO OTHERS BETTER THAN YOU EXPECT
THEY WILL DO ONTO YOU

HONOR VETERANS

LEAD BY EXAMPLE

SERVE CHOCOLATE FOR BREAKFAST

PRAYER IS YOUR PATH TO GOD

BE GRATEFUL

HAVE COMPASSION FOR PEOPLE AND THE PLANET

KNOW RIGHT FROM WRONG AND YOU WILL RISE WHEN THE BELL RINGS

YOU AND ME, WE'LL MAKE THE WORLD BETTER

These are just some of the words. There are so many you can't count them all, and many more hidden behind other leaves that you hope to see in time. And you realize as you look at the roots, the trunk, and the leaves that these are all one. Each concept is a single pane of stained glass, but together they form a luminous painting. Just like a tree in nature, no part of it can exist without the rest. The wisdom ingrained in each leaf lives because it's connected to the sturdy trunk of being there, and the trunk and leaves are fed by love rooted in family, friends, and community.

At first glance, much of what grows on the wisdom tree may appear obvious or even trite. It's not a revelation to see that being kind matters. This is why it's essential to embrace the *active* form of compassion espoused by the Dalai Lama. There is a huge gulf between knowing something is true and putting it into practice on a daily basis. Buckminster (Bucky) Fuller, the futurist best known for inventing the geodesic dome, once wrote that God is a verb. The dictionary defines wisdom as a noun, synonymous with qualities such as keen insight, good judgment, and an accumulated philosophical learning. Borrowing from Bucky, if we reframe wisdom as a verb it becomes far more powerful. It's wisdoming. These days I base my success not on how much money

I've made but on the number of times I do nice things for others and they say to me, "That was kind of you."

As I progressed on my *Good Grandpa* journey, the image of the wisdom tree gradually formed in my mind, or—to put it more accurately—I could more clearly see a tree that has always been there, as if it had been shrouded in an impenetrable fog. For me, what led to the clearing of the mist was the simple act of talking with people. And this has led me to see my own number one thing, the most important leaf of wisdom I can offer: *Find a reason to talk with people, especially those who you might think are different from you.*

Again and again in my conversations I not only learned wonderful new things, I found common ground. And I found this commonality with people who at first appeared to be from different worlds. If I hadn't talked with Rabbi Chaim Prus, I would not have known that he and I began our adult lives in Crown Heights and met our wives there—nor would I see the need for moral teachings as clear as a bell. My conversations with veterans completely transformed my understanding of service and why it's essential to lead by example. I learned that a Muslim imam and I both give chocolate to our grandchildren, and that his teachings are an heirloom passed down, teacher to teacher, from Muhammed and the Angel Gabriel. I learned that grandmas drive hot sports cars and speak comforting words from the cockpits of helicopters. I saw the connection between the migration of monarch butterflies and supporting our grandchildren on their own journeys. And I learned something seriously smart from the proverbial Minister of Silly Walks: I should never conclude with certainty that I know the truth about any of this. The quest for the Holy Grail is the quest for truth. My journey continues. (If you see a tall old man banging coconuts together as he "rides" through the woods, be sure to say hello. We'll have a good conversation.)

It's also important to understand that the wisdom tree is natural. Dr. Samra's family, like yours and mine, *implants* wisdom that grows over time. Trees require nurturing and sunlight. We humans have a lot more in common with the natural world than most people realize; we are, after all, a product of the Earth. We rise up from seeds, live our lives, and return to the Earth sooner or later. The more time we spend in natural settings the more we become attuned to other voices—song-chirping birds, buzzing insects, the whisper of leaves in the wind, a chorus of rushing water—and if we stop and think and really listen we start to hear what is being said. We come to feel that all these living things are an extension of our family, distant cousins perhaps, but family nevertheless. Even rocks, the stoics of the forest, have something to say; just be sure if you feel the call of nature that the rock is actually a rock.

The wisdom tree that I found is just one of many. After all, I'm just one guy, and I've met with only a few people. I'm very curious what would happen if thousands or millions of people set out on their own journey to talk with others from all walks of life. So much could be found to benefit our children. By comparison, the tree I discovered would be a mere seedling in a majestic sea of sequoias.

And what of America and our current troubles? Having more conversations—substantive, honest, and respectful—can open the door to overcoming division and finding hope. Let's start by recognizing that the whole red state/blue state concept was created to generate cable TV ratings. Some might dismiss me as a blue state "lib," to which I would reply that I've never met someone in a red state I didn't like—*once I actually talked with them.* I recall an Uber ride when I was in Florida on business. It was right when there was a bruhaha going on about a transgender influencer who'd appeared in an ad campaign for Bud Light. Kid Rock, a musician known for his conservative views, was shooting cans of Bud Light with an AR-15. As soon as my Uber driver found out I was from New England he asked, "So, do you drink Bud Light?" He appeared to be fishing for an opportunity to have a culture war argument. As it happens, I've never enjoyed any type of light beer and couldn't care less about an ad campaign for one. And how someone identifies their gender is none of my business. Live and let live. I took a deep breath and talked my driver off his culture war ledge by switching the topic to the Boston Celtics, inarguably the best team in basketball, and soon we were having a fun conversation. He was astonished when I gave him a tip.

I realized something else important as I progressed with the book. My original goal was to aggregate wisdom to help nurture the next great generation. Yet I never actually defined what it means to be great. The mythology of the greatest generation that Tom Brokaw wrote about was largely defined by the courage of the soldiers at Normandy. We rightly celebrate their heroism. What we've paid less attention to is the fact that these same fighters gave chocolate bars to children all across Europe. We've seen movies featuring American GIs fighting and dying in Vietnam, yet there is no *Apocalypse Now* showing these men giving toys to the orphans in Hue. (I sure hope there will be.) Unfortunately, kindness doesn't sell tickets.

All this leads me to conclude that one of the most essential hallmarks of greatness for the next generation will not be the scaling of cliffs under machine gun fire but having the wisdom needed to prevent wars from starting in the first place. It took serving in two world wars for my grandfather to conclude that it was always the old men who started wars and the young men who were sent off to fight them. We need today's young men and women to know what our grandfathers learned the hard way. The next time an old man fabricates some BS reason to attack another country, let him be put on the front lines.

The threat of war is only one of the many existential crises our grandchildren face. There's not just one bell ringing. It's a deafening tintinnabulation—from climate change, to pandemics, to political chaos, to AI and whatever future tech Frankenstein is birthed. The sheer number of challenges can appear overwhelming, a heavy paralyzing burden. Yet the beauty of cultivating a forest of wisdom trees is that it will provide our grandchildren with the foundational skills required to solve the toughest problems. They may struggle mightily as they tackle the twenty-first-century versions of the cliffs of Normandy, and they may fall again and again, but in the end their greatness will be evident when they get back up and succeed. I believe they will.

When I was a teenager, I always enjoyed watching *On the Road with Charles Kuralt*, a TV show where Kuralt—a warm and friendly middle-aged newsman with a comb-over—traveled around to visit with people in small-town America and tell their stories. At the end of each segment he always had a great wrap-up, poetic and heartfelt without being smarmy. As I approach the end of my *Good Grandpa* road trip, I will attempt to channel my inner Charles Kuralt with the following summation...

Picture me in a plane looking out the window. I turn to you and begin: "Here, as the warm dusk falls in the world below across the Great Plains, I think of the letter my father wrote to his sons in 1956 on his plane trip across this same America, a letter filled with hope and promise for our country. He urged us to question authority, to ask WHY! And he said the answers could be found through the invincible power of clear thinking. In the course of writing this book, I have been fortunate to hear the clear thoughts of grandfathers—and my aunt Lois—who shared their wonderful life stories and wisdom. This has changed me. My jaded veneer has been—at least to some extent—melted, illuminated by a warm focus of ideas that burn too brightly for my cynicism to withstand. I am full of hope. It is brimming from my full cup.

To my grandchildren reading this—my forever book—I have a time capsule message. At present, you may be entirely preoccupied with fitting together LEGO pieces to make your Mars rover or putting dresses on your Elsa doll. But when you reach the age of understanding, please know that all the problems in the world can be solved, and you have the power within you to make anything happen. You have a voice. Use it! Never take your freedom for granted. The Statue of Liberty is not some random tourist attraction in New York Harbor, not a relic of the past. It's the future—a living, vibrant, towering beacon of freedom shimmering across the waters! Go there. Read the words on the plaque at its base. And while you're waiting in line to go inside, strike up a few conversations with strangers.

If in any way what I have shared in this book helps you live your best life, if it helps you serve others to the fullest, pass it on. Wisdom truly is the best heirloom. Someday—if you are very, very lucky—you will hold a newborn grandchild in your arms. You will feel a sense of total peace and contentment, a love that fills the room and all the world around you. That's how I will always feel when I think of you.

Love,

Grandpa Ted

CHAPTER 24

Dreaming Goodbye

It's only fitting that my final chapter should feature a story told to me by my aunt Lois, since she appeared at the beginning—bookends, if you will. And what she shared with me in this story demonstrates that some things never really end. Love and family have a way of carrying on.

I picture Lois now down by the Willoughby shore on a late summer day, the wind blowing in from the south to make the white-topped waves roll and rumble against the beach. When she starts to tell the story, she's transformed in my mind to how she was in 1939, tall and beautiful with long, wavy red hair.

Lois was in her senior year of high school in Belmont, Massachusetts, and friends with a boy a little older than her. His name was Willard Haskell. Lois had a feeling he was "sweet on her," but he was shy; somehow he'd never managed to ask her out. When the Second World War began, however, Willard found the courage to enlist in the air force. He'd always wanted to be a pilot, and this was his chance. The only problem was that Willard wasn't good at math, and he was worried he wouldn't pass the tough air force exam. He turned to Lois for help, and she tutored him for months. It worked. Willard got into the air force and was shipped off to England. Lois and Willard exchanged a few letters, but gradually they lost touch as the war stretched on into years.

Then one night in early summer as Lois slept in the family homestead just up from the shore of the lake, she had a vivid dream. She was standing on the roof of her high school, looking up, and the entire sky as far as the eye could see was full of American bombers, their wings tip to tip, sheet-metal rivets gleaming in the early morning light.

And there, leaning out the cockpit window of one bomber, was none other than Willard Haskell. He was smiling at her, and waving, his long red scarf fluttering behind. The world shook from the roar of the engines, so intense Lois could feel the roof beneath her bare feet vibrating. And suddenly she was awake.

Lois went downstairs, where my grandmother was in the kitchen making breakfast. "You'll never believe the dream I had," Lois told her. "It was so real." My Gram listened, shaking her head at the story. "Well, isn't that something!"

A short time later, the mailman came by, all excited. "Did you hear the news?" he asked. "The Allies have landed at Normandy. It's D-Day!" They turned on the radio to hear the whole story. So long expected, news of the invasion was thrilling and overwhelming, to the point where Lois's dream fell to the back of her mind.

But two weeks later they heard more news. Willard Haskell was missing in action and presumed dead, his bomber shot down over Normandy on the morning of the invasion. The same morning that Lois had the dream.

Lois never once in all her telling of the story said that Willard Haskell's spirit had come to her to say one final goodbye after his plane, riddled with holes and trailing smoke and flame like his rippling red scarf, rammed into the roiling waves of the English Channel. A goodbye that could not be done with a phone call. Or a letter. There was no time, of course, no possible 1944 technology. Only in a dream could such a swift message be conveyed, instantly, across continents, faster than wind or clouds, as Lois lay asleep, her red hair fanned across a white pillow on the top floor of a peaceful Vermont farmhouse. Only with eyes closed could Willard be seen, waving one final time.

When I checked with the Department of Veterans Affairs to confirm Willard Haskell's fate, and I related Lois's story, they said, "You would be amazed how often we've heard of this happening. First a dream, then they get the call or the telegram."

This made me dig a little deeper into the nature of dreams. It turns out that in Native American cultures there is a widespread belief that in a certain period of dreaming, in that space between deep night sleep and the slow climb toward waking, spirits can visit us. It's the time just before the dawn, before eyelids let in daylight, before the flights of imagination have fully come down to earth, a kind of in-between place; and sometimes—with startling and vivid clarity—we see a husband or wife, a mother or father, a grandparent. They touch our hand and whisper in our ear that they are all right. That we will be all right. That they love us. There at that rare and brief moment, with all the worries of life behind them, they come softly to us and dream their goodbyes. And when we wake, we wonder if it really happened, and we tell our family and our friends, and they shake their heads in wonder with us, and we say that we'll never really know the truth. But deep down, we know. Deep down, when we dream.

Lois sits looking out at the water, her eyes invisible behind her big-framed pink 1970s sunglasses. Seagulls are swooping close to shore, some hovering in the wind, white wings over the blue sky. And when I ask Lois if maybe, just maybe, this vivid dream she can't ever forget was Willard Haskell's spirit saying goodbye, she just makes a "tsk" sound and scoffs, "Well, I don't know about *that*."

EPILOGUE

Dear Twenty-Six-Year-Old Us

Last week my wife was cleaning out an old cabinet and came across a photo taken of us on our honeymoon in London. I'd always liked this picture and thought it had been lost, so seeing it again was a bit like finding ourselves the way we were back then. But not so long ago, really, in terms of years.

The span of time is more accurately measured in the changes we've been through; raising two children and all the blurred rush that entailed; and most recently, the addition of five gregarious and beautiful grandchildren. It wasn't always easy getting to the present. This made me wish I could reach out to the two of us as we were at twenty-six and offer some sage advice.

So, here is my letter to the younger us:

Dear Ted and Nancy...

First off, I'd have to say the two of you look great. Nancy, the combination of the long wavy hair and lovely features makes you stunning. Ted, I know that you are insecure about your looks and have never felt 100 percent comfortable in your skin. Stop worrying.

Nancy and me on our honeymoon in London, 1985.

I want you both to know that you are just at the very beginning of an amazing journey together. It's going to happen very quickly. Nancy, you may already be pregnant, and a little girl named Abigail will join us in nine months. And within three years we will have a son, Nicholas, who will complete the picture.

Your early years as a family will sometimes be rocky to say the least.

There will be a lot of juggling of work and day care, which will be made harder by the fact that both your kids will be sick *a lot*. Not life-threatening sick, but one cold or stomach bug after the other. You will argue about which of you will stay home to care for the kids when they have a fever. You will strike bargains with each other. You will work it out time and again, and the kids will grow up to be well-rounded and charming people.

When times are tough, and when they are great, try to pause and take stock of where you are and appreciate your many gifts. All of it will go by so fast that when you're older you'll shake your head in wonder.

I'd love to go back to one of those bad days and give you a hug. I'd tell you that it's all going to be OK. That's not some platitude; it's the truth.

I wish I could help you pause time once in a while. After you've read to the kids in bed and they fall asleep, don't rush out of the room. Take a moment to look at your slumbering Abigail and Nicholas. Experience deeply the sense of peace. Listen to the sound of their breathing. Realize that these seconds are incredibly precious and transitory. Someday—despite all the vomit you have to clean up on a regular basis, the tears to soothe, and all the other troubles—you will wish you could be right back here in this moment.

Here's some advice about your relationship.

It would be nice if you had more regular dates. Find a sitter and go out to dinner at least twice a month. You don't have to go to a gourmet restaurant. Maybe just have coffee. Take a few minutes to talk. You'll be the best possible parents if you nurture your relationship to the fullest.

When the kids leave for college and you are alone in your newly empty nest, it's OK to feel very sad. Go ahead and bawl your eyes out. So much of your purpose has been centered on raising your girl and boy. The fact that they are now grown up and strong is a sign you did a great job.

This may shock you, but it actually won't be very long before your kids have kids. Honestly, it will feel like you blinked and suddenly there will be a bunch of grandchildren to hug and read to and make cookies with. The empty nest will be full again before you know it.

Lastly, I'd suggest you extend your honeymoon by at least a few weeks. Drive not only through the British Midlands and Wales, but also to Scotland. Go to the northernmost castle on the coast and feel the wind in your hair. A wonderfully rich and busy life with children and grandchildren is before you, but there's no need to rush ahead. Not today. Slow down and enjoy the view, and each other.

Finis

Resources of Note

Grandpas United

https://www.facebook.com/GrandpasUnited/

Grandpas United is a nonprofit organization based in White Plains, New York. Their mission is to utilize the talents, skills, and experiences of grandpas to improve their community. They serve as male role models and mentors through programs that enhance the growth and development of our youth—and by all accounts it's working. I had a great conversation with their leadership, and they reported excellent results, including a drop in crime and fewer at-risk youth getting caught up in the criminal justice system. They also have the best tagline: We're Gramps, Not Grumps! At present, Grandpas United is a regional organization, but I have hope that they will become national and international.

The Long Distance Grandparent

https://thelongdistancegrandparent.com/

Many grandparents struggle with the reality that their grandkids live far away in other states or countries. Bonding with the grandkids and making a difference in their lives can be difficult. Kerry Byrne, PhD, founder of The Long Distance Grandparent, is here to help. She offers a comprehensive range of science-based methodologies to help grandparents stay connected, such as regular mailings and tips for using texts and FaceTime to forge stronger relationships.

Grandparents Academy

https://www.grandparentsacademy.com/

The mission of Grandparents Academy is to help grandparents grow meaningful relationships and rich legacies with their loved ones. They provide a range of master classes and host events aimed at helping us make the most of this amazing life experience.

F3

https://f3nation.com/

The fitter we are as grandpas, the more we can be there for our families. That's where F3 can help (retired air force general Ralph Jodice, featured in this book, is a member). Their mission is to plant, grow, and serve small workout groups for men for the invigoration of male community leadership.

Roots for Boots

https://rootsforboots.com/

Roots for Boots is a nonprofit that helps organize support services for veterans in need. They provide opportunities for community members to use their gifts, talents, and resources to assist in helping our servicemen and women. In short, these veterans served our country. Roots for Boots makes it easier for us to serve them back.

The *Cool Grandpa* Podcast

https://cool-grandpa.us/

Host Greg Payne has interviewed dozens of grandpas from all walks of life, and he does a great job. If you want to delve deeper into the grandpa experience, be sure to check it out.

Really! I'm a Grandparent Podcast

https://podcasts.apple.com/us/podcast/really-im-a-grandparent/id1526876861

Hosted by James Lott Jr, this podcast features a different side of grandparenthood—the growing number of men and women who became grandparents in their thirties and forties.

Endnotes

1 Chapter 3. "Hobbes' Philosophy of Science," *Stanford Encyclopedia of Philosophy*, March 8, 2019, updated June 5, 2023, https://plato.stanford.edu/entries/hobbes-science/.

2 Chapter 3. "The Evolution of Grandparents," *Scientific American*, November 1, 2012, https://www.scientificamerican.com/article/the-evolution-of-grandparents-2012-12-07/.

3 Chapter 10. "Ethical Will," *Wikipedia*, https://en.wikipedia.org/wiki/Ethical_will.

4 Chapter 10. Maureen Stanley, "1900–2000: Changes In Life Expectancy In The United States," SeniorLiving.org, updated October 4, 2024, https://www.seniorliving.org/history/1900-2000-changes-life-expectancy-united-states/.

5 Chapter 11. "Future of jobs 2023: These are the most in-demand skills now – and beyond," World Economic Forum, May 1, 2023, https://www.weforum.org/stories/2023/05/future-of-jobs-2023-skills/.

6 Chapter 12. "The Importance of Social Security Benefits to the Income of the Aged Population," Social Security Administration, https://www.ssa.gov/policy/docs/ssb/v77n2/v77n2p1.html#:~:text=We%20find%20that%20about%20half,percent%20of%20their%20family%20income.

7 Chapter 12. "What young workers should know about Social Security and saving," Social Security Administration, https://www.ssa.gov/newsletter/Statement%20Insert%2025+.pdf.

8 Chapter 13. Anthony Martinez and Cheridan Christnacht, "Women Making Gains in STEM Occupations but Still Underrepresented," United States Census Bureau, January 26, 2021, https://www.census.gov/library/stories/2021/01/women-making-gains-in-stem-occupations-but-still-underrepresented.html.

9 Chapter 14. "The Six Grandfathers Before It Was Known as Mount Rushmore." Native Hope, July 4, 2022, https://blog.nativehope.org/six-grandfathers-before-it-was-known-as-mount-rushmore.

10 Chapter 15. "Child Mortality Rates Plunge by More Than Half Since 1990 but Global MDG Target Missed by Wide Margin," World Bank Group, September 8, 2015, https://www.worldbank.org/en/news/press-release/2015/09/09/child-mortality-rates-plunge-by-more-than-half-since-1990-but-global-mdg-target-missed-by-wide-margin.

11 Chapter 15. "Poverty in India," *Wikipedia*, https://en.wikipedia.org/wiki/Poverty_in_India#:~:text=Bardhan%20also%20concluded%20that%20Indian,and%20not%20doing%20well%20either.

12 Chapter 15. "Poverty rate in India [2024]: Trend over the years and causes," *Forbes India*, October 17, 2024, https://www.forbesindia.com/article/explainers/poverty-rate-in-india/90117/1#:~:text=According%20to%20research%20by%20the,well%20as%20historical%20growth%20rates.

13 Chapter 15. "75 years, 75 % literacy: India's long fight against illiteracy," *The Times of India*, August 14, 2022, https://timesofindia.indiatimes.com/india/75-years-75-literacy-indias-long-fight-against-illiteracy/articleshow/93555770.cms.

14 Chapter 15. "Ways We Can Improve the Literacy Rate in India in 2023," Cyboard School, https://cyboardschool.com/ways-we-can-improve-literacy-rate-in-india-2023/#:~:text=According%20to%20the%20latest%20data,%2C%20with%20an%20impressive%2096.2%25.

15 Chapter 19. Matt Murphy in London and Daniel Pardo in Bogota, "How children survived 40 days in Colombian jungle," BBC News, June 12, 2023, https://www.bbc.com/news/world-europe-65871238.

16 Chapter 19. Rodger Desai, "Ensuring Online Safety: The Challenges and Solutions of Age Verification for Kids," *Forbes*, October 2, 2024, https://www.forbes.com/councils/forbestechcouncil/2024/10/02/ensuring-online-safety-the-challenges-and-solutions-of-age-verification-for-kids/.

17 Chapter 19. Jamie Waters, "Constant craving: how digital media turned us all into dopamine addicts," *The Guardian*, August 22, 2021, https://www.theguardian.com/global/2021/aug/22/how-digital-media-turned-us-all-into-dopamine-addicts-and-what-we-can-do-to-break-the-cycle.

18 Chapter 19. Caroline Miller, "Does Social Media Use Cause Depression?" Child Mind Institute, October 31, 2024, https://childmind.org/article/is-social-media-use-causing-depression/.

19 Chapter 19. "In our digital world, are young people losing the ability to read emotions?" UCLA Health, August 21, 2014, https://www.uclahealth.org/news/release/people-losing-ability-to-read-emotions#:~:text=%E2%80%

9CIf%20you're%20not%20practicing,need%20device%2Dfree%20 time.%E2%80%9D.

20 Chapter 19. "Landmark Report: U.S. Teens Use an Average of Nine Hours of Media Per Day, Tweens Use Six Hours," Common Sense Media, November 3, 2015, https://www.commonsensemedia.org/press-releases/landmark-report-us-teens-use-an-average-of-nine-hours-of-media-per-day-tweens-use-six-hours.

21 Chapter 19. Nsikan Akpan, "Toddlers' screen time linked to slower speech development, study finds," PBS News, May 4, 2017, https://www.pbs.org/newshour/health/toddlers-screen-time-linked-slower-speech-development-study-finds.

22 Chapter 19. "Human multitasking," *Wikipedia*, https://en.wikipedia.org/wiki/Human_multitasking#:~:text=Human%20multitasking%20is%20the%20concept,phone%20while%20driving%20a%20car.&text=Multitasking%20can%20result%20in%20time,attention%20divided%20among%20different%20tasks.

23 Chapter 19. Gloria Mark, Daniela Gudith, and Ulrich Klocke, "The Cost of Interrupted Work: More Speed and Stress," University of California, Irvine, https://ics.uci.edu/~gmark/chi08-mark.pdf.

24 Chapter 19. "Devices in the Classroom," Harvard University, The Derek Bok Center for Teaching and Learning, https://bokcenter.harvard.edu/technology-and-student-distraction.

25 Chapter 19. Veronika Marek, et al. "Blue light phototoxicity toward human corneal and conjunctival epithelial cells in basal and hyperosmolar conditions," *Free Radical Biology and Medicine*, vol. 126 (October 2018): 27–40, https://pubmed.ncbi.nlm.nih.gov/30040995/.

26 Chapter 19. F. Behar-Cohen, et al. "Light-emitting diodes (LED) for domestic lighting: any risks for the eye?" *Progress in Retinal and Eye Research*, vol. 30, no. 4 (July 2011): 239–257, https://pubmed.ncbi.nlm.nih.gov/21600300/.

Acknowledgments

Writing is often seen as a solitary craft. It certainly can be, but in my case the engine of my creativity was the involvement of many great people; they may not have been with me at my desk, but they built the invaluable connections—in the physical world and in my brain—that wove my rough literary fabric into a tapestry. I will do my best here to thank them.

First and foremost, my wife, Nancy, was always there for me to review early drafts and offer up suggestions. She also managed to put up with my very loud typing, which too often woke her up before the sun rose above the Vermont mountains. My children, Abigail and Nicholas, are a constant source of inspiration. My growing brood of grandchildren—like baby dinosaurs who've escaped from Jurassic Park—bring their own brand of delightful mayhem to my doorstep. Thank you.

Paul Bresnick, my literary agent, contacted me out of the blue and suggested I write the book. I'm thankful to Paul as well as the dozens of publishers who passed on the book, because ultimately the right publisher, Gretchen Young of Regalo Press, said yes.

Kristin Collins did a wonderful job designing the cover for the book. And Doug Feinburg was a huge help producing videos for book promotion. Thank you both.

Author and Harvard professor Eric McNulty took the time to have coffee with me to talk about the power of conversations to overcome division. I hope more people have a chance to read his books. Thanks, Eric.

There was a fair amount of research required, from tracking down dangerous Amazonian species, to learning Native American perspectives on grandparenthood, and much more. Veronika Moroz was a big help with all of it. Thanks.

Getting connected to grandpas to interview was not easy. When I reached out to grandpas as a total stranger, I often felt like the old man in Coleridge's *Rime of the Ancient Mariner* who "stoppeth one of three" and was met with "By thy long grey beard and glittering eye, now wherefore stopp'st thou me?" As you can imagine, most of my emails didn't garner a response. The only way to make a good connection was through personal contacts, which is why I owe a deep debt of gratitude to all the friends and family who reached out to their contacts on my behalf. I called these folks my *Good Grandpa* co-conspirators. They include, not shown here in order of importance, the following kind souls:

Paula Span, a *New York Times* columnist who connected me with Jennifer Brokaw, who then connected me with her dad; my brother, Nick, for his introduction to Eric Behr; Scott Galin, who connected me with two wonderful rabbis, Chaim Prus and Eric Gurvis; my wife's cousin, Susan Carpenter, who introduced me to Father Craig Burlington (who in turn introduced me to Dr. Abdul Hamid Samra); Tenzin Taklha, personal secretary to the Dalai Lama, who asked His Holiness for his number one wisdom on my behalf; the Lexington Veterans Association made an introduction to Gresh Lattimore; Greg Payne, producer and host of the *Cool Grandpa* podcast, introduced me to several wonderful grandpas, including Ralph Jodice and James Lott Jr.; Bob Abate introduced me to the story of Bob Staranowicz; Jess

Stone-Weaver introduced me to her father in law, Buck Weaver; Dr. Jing Liu opened up his WeChat "Rolodex" to the local Chinese community; Louise Fernandez, the little sister I never had, wisely suggested I talk with her boyfriend, Fred Schoch; Jim Isenberg and Frank Williams—leaders of Grandpas United—united me with Reggie Williams.

When I spoke with Dr. Samra, an imam, he said we should never turn away anyone who seeks to learn from us. That principle was evident in all the great people who took the time to share their insights with me. My dear departed aunt Lois White got the ball rolling with her sage advice. To all the grandpas who shared their stories and wisdom with me, I cannot thank you enough.

Last but not least, I thank God, who I got to know better in the course of writing the book.

About the Author

Ted Page is a storyteller and performer. His nonfiction stories have appeared in *Boston Magazine* and the *Boston Globe Magazine,* and his comedy screen credits include work with John Cleese and Florence Henderson. His blog for grandfathers—GoodGrandpa.com—has been featured in *The New York Times.* Ted's book of true family stories, *The Willoughby Chronicles,* was published in 2017. Ted is a founding partner of Captains of Industry, a leading boutique marketing consultancy, and a graduate of the University of Massachusetts, Amherst. He lives in New England and has a bunch of grandchildren.